Social Media
in the Classroom

Social Media in the Classroom

Why Ontario Students Are Failing in the Real World

JASON BEAUDRY

iUniverse, Inc.
Bloomington

Social Media in the Classroom
Why Ontario Students Are Failing in the Real World

iUniverse books may be ordered through booksellers or by contacting:

iUniverse
1663 Liberty Drive
Bloomington, IN 47403
www.iuniverse.com
1-800-Authors (1-800-288-4677)

ISBN: 978-1-4759-5978-9 (sc)
ISBN: 978-1-4759-5980-2 (hc)
ISBN: 978-1-4759-5979-6 (ebk)

Library of Congress Control Number: 2012921350

Printed in the United States of America

iUniverse rev. date: 11/14/2012

Contents

Preface

I was in my late twenties when I decided to go back to school and get my bachelor of arts degree. I had the full intention of applying to the bachelor of education program once I completed my first degree. When it was all said and done, I had a bachelor of arts degree in history and English with a minor in classics. My son, Braden, was born in 1998, and I knew I needed to do something with my life that he could be proud of. I registered at Nipissing University in the fall of 1999 and began classes on a part-time basis in January 2000 while working full-time at a local call centre. Braden was just under two years old, and I wanted to do something that would allow me to provide for him. Prior to that, I had a few menial jobs that did not satisfy me nor give me any pleasure—emotionally or financially. I had the grand idea of going to school and making a difference, because if I was not going to make a difference, then why bother?

My first teaching job was on an isolated First Nation reserve, and as sad as I was to be away from my son, I am glad I went, because I got to meet some great people along the way—specifically Ron Pate and Lindy Kataquapit. Ron Pate was the principal there, and he was extremely supportive of his teachers. Maybe that was a bad thing to experience in my first teaching job, because I was set up to believe that was how it would be all the time. He cared for his students as much as he cared for his teachers, and he treated everyone equitably—even though it was not always reciprocated, as the education authority would often blame him for whatever was going on. As bad as he was often treated, he always smiled and took it with a grain of salt because he was in the business of educating children and not appeasing the education authority and their agendas. For those who do not know, the education authority is the equivalent of a school board, just on a smaller scale. His life could have been much easier if he had just done what the education authority demanded of him. Nevertheless, that is not how Ron conducted his education policy. He had high expectations of his teachers and his students even though it went against what the education authority demanded. Ron Pate, you are a true educator and an even better leader. You did what was best for your students and your teachers as opposed to what was best for the authority. I would like to thank you for the opportunity you gave me. Lindy, you made me feel like I was part of the community. You were always willing to help me out and were there to chat hockey with me. You are a true gentleman and a great friend. I wish you and your family all the best.

After I left Attawapiskat, I went on to work for the Near North District School Board, and I absolutely love the school where I have taught for the last number of years. I enjoy working with the students, and they will forever be a part of me wherever my career leads me. They are a huge part of my inspiration for writing this book. If I did not care about their future I would have not bothered taking the time to write this.

The reason why I chose to write this book is simply because it was the right thing to do regardless of what the powers that be believe. This is for the Lynden Dorvals out there. I know it is controversial and many people will not like what is being said within the pages of this book, but it needs to be said. When I was asked who my target market would be, the simple answer was "Everyone!" This book was written for parents, teachers, school administrators, the Ministry of Education and the Provincial government. Our education system has been going in the wrong direction; we all know it, and we all see it, but very little is being done to get it back on track. The lack of action could be because school administrators and teachers know they will be putting their careers in jeopardy if they speak up, and for that reason this book needs to be written. My hope is that this book will get people talking and hopefully demand a change to our current education system that is in shambles. We cannot allow this trend to continue.

I am a teacher and forever will have the passion to teach; this book may hurt my chances of doing that, as principals will likely shy away from offering me any other posts in the future because of what I wrote here. However, as much as principals have the power to run their own schools, they have bosses they have to follow. I speak from the trenches, as I am there and have been there to see how our educational system is misleading our children in preparing them for their futures. I entered the profession to make a difference, and for the last few years, the direction our educational system is heading has really forced me to rethink my ideology of making a difference. I am not alone in this frustration; many great teachers share my sense of defeat because we have our hands tied as a result of political rhetoric that prevents us from properly educating Ontario's children. I am a passionate teacher who cares for his students like so many other teachers. The problem is that politics has had its collective arms in our classrooms, interfering with our ability to prepare Ontario's students for the future. There is far too much bureaucracy in the education profession, and these bureaucrats come up with initiative after initiative that does very little in progressing the cognitive development of our children. It actually does more harm than good. What is important to the Ministry of Education is simply the numbers. They force the hands of school administrators to enforce certain policies onto principals and teachers to increase credits earned and graduation rates at all costs. It does not matter that students are not properly prepared as long as they get their credits and obtain their Ontario Secondary School Diploma, because the bottom line is what matters, not the journey to get there. I am not saying I have all the answers, but together as parents and teachers we can start making the changes necessary for the children of this province. When parents and teachers work together it will force principals and senior administrators to hear the voice of reason and take it up the ladder of our educational system. Let's make a difference for our children. They are worth it! Our voices need to be heard!

What I am suggesting throughout these pages is to bring to light to what is going on within our educational walls. We need to stand up and demand better for our children. We need to enforce some modicum of discipline with our children in our schools. This will start changing their mindset about their education. We have to bring back accountability within the education system, and once there, it will make a difference in the importance of the educational process in this province. The lack of student accountability is appalling, and our children know this, so why would they see their education as something of importance when there is a lack of accountability? Let's expect more from our "Education Premier" Dalton McGuinty and improve this system that has potential to be great. We have to demand greatness to achieve greatness.

Thank you. I hope you enjoy reading this book as much as I enjoyed writing it.

Jason Beaudry

Acknowledgments

I would like to thank Dr. Colleen Franklin who gave me guidance along my journey. She was always there helping me reach my goals. Her advice was invaluable. Thank you for taking the time to read this and giving me a vote of confidence to publish. Also, Colleen Kleven for sitting with me to discuss avenues I could take as well as pointing me in the iUniverse direction.

I would also like to thank my mother, Denise Beaudry, for making this happen without her this would not have been possible. Special thanks go out to my beautiful wife Josie who gave me the confidence to do this, and of course to our children because they are our future. This is for the passionate teachers like Marilyn Collins, Brigitte Raymond Laing, and Lynden Dorval among many others.

I would also like to extend a big thank you to my good friend Brian Lebid who did the final editing of this book. Your advice and expertise was greatly appreciated.

Jason Beaudry

Introduction

The picture on the previous page speaks volumes in terms of the direction of our current educational system in Ontario. I am sure similar problems lie outside of Ontario; however, I will focus specifically on the issues of this province. There was a time when parents and teachers were on the same page when it came to the success or failure of our Ontario students. Back in the "glory days" students had to complete their work to the best of their ability in order to achieve a passing grade. If they did not they were held back. Completing homework and studying to earn a passing grade in today's schools is such an antiquated way of thinking. Sadly, it is not solely in Ontario that the idea of no child left behind is construed as a good thing in our schools. This idea has been rampant throughout North America. The irony is that many people agree that there is a problem with our education system; consequently, we just continue to tow the line and do as we are told by our superiors. Teachers follow the rules directed to them by their principals; the principals do as their told by their board's senior administrators which then are directed to follow the Ministry of Education's political mandate. We need to take the politics out of our schools and educate for the sake of our children's future and not for any political purposes.

In 2011, Ontario's Premier Dalton McGuinty proudly stated that 81% of Ontario secondary school students were graduating high school; however, it does not really illustrate an accurate picture of how it is in this province. I am not sure if the powers that be actually believe in the direction our education system has gone and continues to go, but the one aspect that must be observed is that the youth of this province are the ones getting the short end of the educational stick. The Ministry of Education's ideology of no child left behind has done a far greater disservice to our youth by trying not to hurt their feelings and lower their self-esteem then to have them redo a grade when and if needed. Our children's self-esteem was the reason why the policy was implemented. Children would avoid having to repeat a grade and feeling bad that they were not successful and will not be with their friends in the following grade. In theory the idea sounds admirable; however, realistically it does far more damage than good. Children who grow up believing that regardless what they do, or do not do, they will still be successful opens the door to complacency and complacency leads to a diminished educational value. Once that box is opened it will be difficult to shut.

I do not profess to have all the answers but I do know something needs to change otherwise in the following years all we will hear is "Our Educational System is broken and needs to be fixed." In my typical proactive thinking I felt it was vital to write this in order to help open the eyes of our leaders, and those in charge of our education system to start thinking of making some changes now before it is too late. That 81% graduation rate of Ontario secondary students may look good on paper, or in the political platform but it says very little when these same students head to college, university or the workforce. These issues do not simply begin in high school, but far earlier even before children enter elementary school because what kids learn at an early age is vital to how they learn later on in their lives. The changes that are needed should not simply begin in high school; I strongly feel that changes need to start at home and then once they enter elementary school they will have that initial start that get them on their way. Parents need to take responsibility for their children's education prior to the beginning of formal schooling. It is common knowledge that a child who is read to prior to formalize schooling has a far greater chance to become successful in school than a child who is not. It is integral that parents take some responsibility in this process as well as help the education system by given their children the tools to be successful in school and beyond. A baby's brain is much like a sponge and whatever that child learns aids in the development of their cognitive thinking process. Jean Piaget's "Theory of Cognitive Development" argues that there are stages to cognitive development and these stages are vital to a child's learning progression. It appears our educational system is getting away from these ideas of helping our youth get the advantage they deserve, the real advantage they need in tomorrow's ever expanding global world.

What is discouraging about today's world is far too many people are always rushing from one place to the next and not taking the time for important aspects in their lives—the family unit. Far too many families are not taking the time to share memorable events such as eating supper together. Too much importance is placed on technological devices such as cell phones and computers. Instead of spending quality time with each other we are running in and out of each other's lives and simply communicating through text messages or on each other's Facebook walls. We, as a society, just allow this type of behaviour to continue which is why there is a fair amount of disconnect in the family life which leads to a definite disconnect within the education system. The focus, for this book, will be more on the adolescent years; however, I fell it is necessary to speak a little about what needs to be done prior to students entering high school.

EDUCATION
BEFORE SCHOOL

The greatest gift a parent can give a child is love and affection and of course—Time. All children, but young children in particular, who spend quality time with their mom and or dad reading together will do so much in assisting their cognitive development. Infants have the ability to soak up all the knowledge that mom or dad is giving them-good or bad. Spending some quality time before bed reading to children provides them a good start for a love of books. It also helps them improve and increase their vocabulary and much more then that they feel their parents love. They get that much valuable quality time with mom and or dad. Too much emphasis had been placed on the television raising our children because we are "too busy." We should never be "too busy" for our children. What we give them early on in life will follow them for the rest of their lives. Checking Facebook, Twitter or whatever else is going on within the confines of social media should never take precedent over our children. Who cares what the Kardashians are doing or specifically not doing; it pales in comparison to what our children are doing or specifically not doing—like their school work. Spending quality family time at an early age will make raising young children and then teenagers a little easier; it is not to say all children will be perfect, but it will not make things worse—remember teaching never ends. Children need to be taught proper behaviour and proper learning. Doing something as simple as reading to our young children will make a world of difference in how they are able to learn when they begin school. However, sadly far too many children do not get the much valuable time with mom and or dad. Far too many children are rarely read to. We as parents need to take responsibility for this. When home life fails the responsibility falls onto the shoulders of our education system and at the moment this system is failing them—maybe not so much at the junior and senior kindergarten levels but more so later on at the elementary and high school years.

JUNIOR AND SENIOR KINDERGARTEN YEARS

One positive course of action the Ontario government has done in terms of improving education was to make full day junior kindergarten. It is a good place to start by providing our youth a reasonable chance to become successful during their educational experience. For the children who do not get valuable learning at home going to school all day will give them the opportunity to get a good start at learning. Our educational system needs to be proactive and help students who are not given the same opportunities at home. In junior and senior kindergarten, children are taught the basics of learning letters, basic words, how to write and of course how to properly interact with one another. They are taught to respect people and things. Junior and senior kindergarten teachers along with early childhood educators are extremely valuable in the educational process because this is where a large portion of our youth get the essential skills they will need to become key members of society. The government needs to place a greater emphasis that all students get the necessary skills needed to progress within their educational careers. Yes, even at the kindergarten level. The earlier we start the better it will be for our children. Each educational level is vital to progress to the next level.

It is essential that kindergarten classrooms be kept within a reasonable range of no more than 20 students per classroom so teachers and early childhood educators can provide the support needed for all our children. Junior and senior kindergarten students need to receive the necessary basis skills in order to be successful in grade 1 through grade 8. This is not to say that simply because children are read to at home and class sizes are kept reasonable will be the key to greatness from all our students. It would be unrealistic to think that, there will always be some students who fall behind and need extra help. In the long term, repeating a grade, if necessary, will be more helpful than harmful. If a student cannot read or do what is expected of them in grade 6 that student will not succeed in grade 7 and beyond so why make their lives more difficult by pushing them along when they do not have the necessary skills or knowledge to succeed at the next level. Taking one step back and repeat a grade to take two steps forward and succeed later on. We do not get a free ride in adulthood, so why set children up for failure and disappointment later on in life?

ELEMENTARY SCHOOL AGE

As important as junior and senior kindergarten years are for the cognitive development of children, elementary school is where they begin to learn the ways of the future in what they can or cannot get away with. This stage of their lives is where they often begin to learn how to manipulate the adults in their lives in order to get their way—that is if adults allow them. There is a term that I learned a few years back from a former colleague called, "train the puppies." It was being used in regards to grade nine students because, as he liked to say, they needed to be "trained" but it can be easily applied to all levels and all students. You have to properly train a puppy to go outside to do its "business," to not bark for nothing, to not run away etc . . . We train puppies to be exactly what we expect of them to do and not do. This same concept should be practiced with children. We need to properly train children just like we would with our puppies. Consequently, we should hold our children in higher regards than puppies, and maintain high expectations of our children that they can be taught and learn to a high degree. We will continuously work with puppies so they get what is expected of them. Unfortunately, we tend to give up far easier with children than we do with puppies. It is understandable that not all students learn the same way and at the same speed. This is understood within the educational system as the catch phrase in Professional Development is differentiated instruction in which students learn differently and should be taught differently. It is believed that teaching so that all students are able to learn to the best of their abilities is essential for their success; however, that in no way means that the educational system should cave to students and parents because of some of their difficulties. Some difficulties can be overcome if everyone involved works together to overcome them. We should focus on what they are having difficulties with (i.e. reading and writing) and help our children overcome such problems; instead of just letting students skate by for fear of hurting their self-esteem and their feelings. Our education, and society for that matter, has fallen into an Oprahfication of doing what feels good and not what is necessarily beneficial for the youth in this province.

Far too many students feel inadequate because of some of their learning issues and simply feel that they are too dumb to learn and wallow in complacency and self-doubt. It is not that they are dumb it is that they were taught at an early age that hard work was not important like it once was. This is not to say this is the fault of teachers, but more of a system problem that allows complacency to occur. Many more students may be graduating from Ontario high schools today than they did twenty years ago, but what is that high school diploma worth if they cannot think for themselves, spell properly or read above a grade 6 level?

In Ontario, many students have Individual Educational Plans or IEP's which if used properly can help students improve. An Individual Education Plan should not just be implemented in order for a school to obtain additional funding. When a student has difficulty reading and has an Individual Education Plan as a result, the educational system should provide additional assistance to help that student learn to read. We should not enable this student by reading for him or her but assist the student to be able to read on their own.

I often use a skateboarding analogy to illustrate my point about reading. When a student says to me that he or she "cannot" read I ask them, "is it that you cannot read or that you simply do not like to read?" and the response I normally get is the latter. There is a huge difference in having the ability to read and the ability to read well—which goes to fluency and comprehension. Many students, for whatever reason, would rather be read to instead of reading themselves which goes back to not placing a greater importance for children to read earlier on in their lives. Why do something for yourself when someone else will do it for you? This is the type of mentality that dominates in our society. They do not want to read because for most of their young lives they did not have to read. It becomes a vicious cycle of complacency which results in someone or something doing the reading for them which just continues and becomes an issue later on. This goes back to an early age if their lack of desire to read was construed as an inability to read therefore leading to an increase push for the creation of Individual Education Plans. In no way am I saying that Individual Education Plans are a waste, just that a large portion of them have been overly misunderstood or taken advantage of for the benefit of the school and not necessarily for the best interest of the students. Individual Education Plans do generate some additional funding for schools; the school receives additional funding to pay for whatever a particular student requires whether it is assistive technology or possibly an Education Assistant. What often occurs is instead of helping a student learn to read and read with fluency and comprehension the heads of our education system have decided to have someone read for them or have some technological device read for them. So what do they learn—if you are not strong at something someone will do it for you instead of teaching you how to do it.

Now to get back to the analogy of skateboarding that I like to use with students. I ask the student the first time he or she got on a skateboard how it felt? They usually respond with something like it was "weird" "scary" or "hard." I ask them if he or she can do the same tricks now as they did when they first got on the skateboard. I ask them what they did to get better and every single time the response is "I kept at it, or I just practiced a lot." I normally finish with so you physically got on the skateboard and did it, tried new things and just kept practicing. You did not just watch a video of it or have someone else do it for you? I usually then smile and say you can do the same with reading or whatever difficulty they may have in school. "Vygotsky said that if you give a child a task to do and he cannot do it, then you have the chance to teach (Wilhelm, 10). This is where the education system is failing because the system would much prefer bring the child along then to teach them to accomplish the task on their own. Sometimes it takes time, and additional assistance which involves time and money when what really matters to the Ministry of Education is the numbers. I understand this will not always work for every student as some have deeper learning issues but for a large portion it will make a world of difference. For the students who still require additional assistance the programs available could be used for these particular students with

Individual Education Plans. I will go in greater detail about IEP's and issues of funding a little later on.

The French child psychologist Jean Piaget (1896-1980) created his four stages of cognitive development that is still relevant today. The four stages are the Sensori-motor (Birth—2 years), Pre-operational (2-7 years), Concrete Operational (7-11 years), and Formal Operational (11 years and up). Children at a young age comprehend what they do and how other's react shapes their understanding of how their world works. Infants understand that when they cry someone will come and either change them, feed them or just hold them. So when they want or need one of these things they understand what they need to do to get what they want and need. They cannot speak so they figure out what they need to do. In Piaget's second period (2-7 years) is what he calls "the Characteristic Behaviour Phase where there is an increase use of verbal representation but speech is egocentric. Whereas when children reach 4-7 years old their speech becomes more social, less egocentric and only uses simple do's and don'ts imposed by authority" ("Learning and Teaching"). This is where we as parents and teachers need to improve; we need to set reasonable and attainable expectations for children and stick with them. Children need to understand that their actions and words have consequences and will no longer be tolerated. They need to be held responsible for their actions regardless how unfair they think it is. Children who lack understanding of consequences and still get praise or rewards when they do not do what is expected of them will only continue to not do as expected of them. This lack of expectations will be what is expected of them. When this occurs, it is they who have trained us as opposed to the other way around. When a student fails to do any of the school work expected of him or her and yet still "earns" a passing grade then that child has discovered that he or she does not have to do any work to be successful in school. The more this happens the more it will happen. Children talk and in today's world of social media the word gets out quick. When children see, and hear that a fellow student did little to no work and still passes then more children will follow. This kind of behaviour will spread like a bad weed. Independent work has been pushed aside in favour of group work so it is easy to see how fast children follow one another. The more it is allowed to happen the more it will happen and then it becomes difficult to stop—which is where we are now.

Piaget's third stage the Period of Concrete Operations (7-12 years) furthers my point by stating that children are able to "organize logical thought and comprehend the principal of conservation" ("Learning and Teaching"). They comprehend what is going on around them and if they see that doing very little will get them similar results to working hard then the majority will chose to do very little work. Why work hard if you do not have to? This in no way suggests that all children are lazy, not at all just that they have learned that little work is expected of them because that was what they learned from an early age. They just continue on the path of complacency. If we expect little from our students we will get exactly what we expect from them.

Class Sizes

The discussion of class size or more appropriately the number of children in a class can lead to very different opinions depending on one's perspective. It is always funny to hear a great number of parents stating how easy teachers have it. How teachers have all those holidays off, and only work until around 3:00 pm everyday with weekends off. However, it is normally these same parents who complain how their 1 or 2 children at home are getting on their nerves during the Christmas holidays or March break and yet they only have 1 or 2 children at home. Teachers have upwards of 24 or more and high school teachers easily have more than sixty students every day. With regards to our youth and our future we need to not just look at the dollars and cents because our place on the global stage will continue to diminish if this trend continues. Ontario's students will no longer be able to compete against Asian and Middle Eastern students because of the lack of support we are providing our Ontario students now and in the near future unless things change for the betterment of our educational system. What the government would save in terms of decreasing support would be lost tenfold by the number of our students not being able to compete in the real world; there will be a brain drain that will affect us substantially leaving irrevocable consequences. We need to maintain a proper cap on each class size. We need to put our trust and faith in our students and provide them with the greatest chance at educational success and if that costs a little more money then so be it because the cost will be far greater if we ignore our youth. The government, by its own admission, stated that class sizes do make a difference in student success. The Liberal government stated, "Since 2003, the government has maintained that smaller classes yield better results through teacher-student interaction" (edu.gov).

By having larger class sizes it simply allows more students to be "left behind" in terms of the educational experience they receive. The idea of "no child left behind" has gone in the wrong direction because as so many are well aware that Ontario's students no longer are expected to repeat a grade regardless of comprehension of curriculum expectations. A child who is pushed along in advancing grades when he or she does not meet expectations is essentially being left behind in their ability to comprehend subject content. The irony is that in the curriculum teachers need to teach all expectations for the subject and students must achieve these expectations; however, whether students do or not do they continue to ascend to the next grade. The Ministry of Education sets curriculum expectations for teachers and students, but really they are more guidelines than expectations because with expectations they should be reached in order to be successful and that is no longer the case with our current education system. These students will be pushed and pulled along without fully grasping educational expectations. This will do far more harm, later on in life, then good. We need to provide our students, all of our students, more teacher—student interaction to increase the chance of our students becoming successful-successful in the ability to comprehend, and not only in the success of credits achieved. If students need more interaction they should be able to get it whether it is from a teacher or at times with an educational assistant. EA's are an integral part of our educational system and yet many are undervalued and often not used properly. I have been witness to Educational Assistants stuffing envelopes and doing menial tasks for the head of the special educational department instead of having them work with high needs students. So with the great number of our students being formally identified it would be believed that class sizes would be restricted to accommodate the needs of our students. At the elementary level, where students are at a key stage of their cognitive development it is vital to get them on track so they do not fall far behind.

In order to ensure we give them the full support they need, class size should not exceed twenty-two students at the elementary level. Ontario's students are worth it and should not be left behind in their development because they are too many students in a class for the teacher to provide the identified students with the additional assistance they are entitled to receive.

The problem that Ontario teachers face every day is the number of identified students in their class. Ontario teachers have to juggle instructional time with providing small group or one-on-one help to the students who require it. What often happens is the teacher focuses on the few high needs students because their Individual Educational Plan (IEP) requires additional assistance. Which is great but depending on the number of identified students in the class it becomes very time consuming and nearly impossible to accommodate. The C and C+ students are not given the assistance they require where they could possibly become B students with a little more attention. The students who usually get left behind are the solid B+ and A students because they are seen as self-sufficient and require little to no assistance. The issue with this ideology is these students become bored and often very disruptive which then leads to classroom management issues that the teacher must deal with. In dealing with classroom management issues the teacher's focus shifts from providing additional assistance to students with IEP's to dealing with behavioural issues. It is these students that become the greatest disrupters because they are left alone so often. These A students begin to lose interests in the system, they start to miss school and become the biggest issue for classroom management because they begin to believe that they are being ignored, where, in turn they seek attention by disrupting the classroom learning. The more disruptions the less instructional time is given. Capping an elementary class to no more than 22 students would help alleviate the behaviours that dominate the attention of teachers. The day could be focused on instructing our students and teaching them to become lifelong learners.

When we ignore our high achievers for too long they cease to be high achievers, or at least high achievers in the sense of high expectations. The students who would and could earn in the high 80s and higher begin to lose interest and see their marks drop in the 70s and low 80s. What often occurs in this situation is teacher's expectations drop as well. What would normally have received in the mid 70s get bumped up to 80s because of teacher's lowered expectations. Instead of having students work hard, do their best and have high expectations of themselves we have allowed them to submit subpar work and view it better than it really is because we, as a society, have grown to expect less than we deserve. We have learned to settle for mediocrity by accepting less than the best from our students which turns into a vicious circle of mediocrity. Today's 80s are more like the low 70s of twenty years ago. Instead of continuing on this path of lowered expectations for our students, we need to move away from the Jersey Shore mentality and begin challenging students again. The Jersey Shore and the Kardashians should never be what we allow our students to strive for; we need to place them in higher regard. We are experiencing a watered down society right now and if we do not stop it, it will get worse. We need to buckle down and make the appropriate changes because our children, our future depends on it. We need to challenge our students instead of allowing subpar work, or no work for that matter, to be the standard that we accept in Ontario's schools. We need to take a stand and initiate a global challenge and strive for the best in today's ever expanding technological world.

The idea of capping class sizes is a great idea; nonetheless, in high school the way the cap size gets circumvented is by the average class size throughout the entire school as opposed to each class. It depends on the actual level because academic and open classes often have numbers in the high 20s to low 30s; whereas, locally developed classes normally have less than 15 students. Consequently, some special needs classes have only a handful of students aiding in the presupposed notion that average class sizes remain "capped" at twenty-four students per classroom. There are always ways school administrators elude policy to cut spending for their own personal agenda—to elevate their status with the board with the hopes of an eventual promotion or at times simply because that is what is expected of them. All principals were once teachers and understand what goes on in the classroom or at least they should understand what is going on; nevertheless, when they aspired for more authority it is like they forgot when they were in the classroom. If they did, chances are they would not do many of the things they do. By having 30 or more students in a classroom it does very little to benefit the students. I do not want to give all principals a bad rap because we all know they have bosses that give them directives that they have to follow. Even though the cap is set at 22 students in high school I have been in a class with as much as 37 students in an open level course. The majority of the time, I have had a minimum of

24 students at an applied level class with up to 30 students in academic classes. Our children are our future, they are the future of this fine province but if this trend continues our future is in peril.

Getting back to cap size in elementary school which is where we should focus because giving students a good start is essential to the well being of our society. If we focused on not accepting mediocrity from our students, early on, it would go a long way in not costing our students in the future and additionally wasting further government's expenditures. If we stop allowing our students to submit subpar work and subpar independent thinking it will save plenty of waste within our government's spending—which seems to be the main focus for Ontario's Liberal government. It is understandable that the government should not be wasting money but our children should not get short changed in favour of cost cutting measures.

Individual Education Plans (IEP)

For a number of years Individual Educational Plans have been in place in Ontario's schools; however, this policy has steadily grown within the Ministry of Education in the last decade or so. The increase use of IEP's in Ontario schools was implemented as a result of a spike in Ontario students with learning concerns. In the past, our education was the same as in how teachers approached the instructional process. The teacher taught and the student listened. The desks were lined single file and that is just how things were. The students were expected to learn as directed without any consideration on the individual student or their individual learning styles which we knew very little about. It was not a big concern on understanding that not all students learn the same. Our students either passed or failed based on these particular teaching strategies. The problem with this form of teaching style is that many students were seen as failures because they lacked the necessary ability to learn in the conventional ways that were being taught. It could easily be argued that we went from one extreme to the next. Years ago the education system did little to understand our students learning needs to doing very little to expect anything but mediocrity from them. We need to find that happy medium.

Ontario students learning issues were becoming more transparent within the confines of our educational walls thus leading to a governmental policy change within the Ministry of Education. This led educated people with fancy suits to implement changes to help a great number of our students with learning concerns overcome such difficulties, by way of Individual Education Plans. IEP's have been around for some time just not readily used or recognized. A greater importance was placed on the policy and thus school boards were expected to fully implement the use of Individual Education Plans in Ontario's schools.

When Individual Education Plans are properly used and correctly implemented they have beneficial purposes for our students with special needs. An IEP is intended to help students attain their educational goals. There are a wide range of reasons why a particular student would have been identified and have an Individual Education Plan. Even though the special education department handle the Individual Education Plan process there is no real negative stigma that students with IEP's are less than any other students.

As was mentioned earlier, if Individual Education Plans are properly implemented and adequately used they can prove beneficial to the student. The special education department along with the school principal are responsible to ensure the implementation of all Individual Education Plans and ensuring that expectations are being followed. It is also in place to assure that students are getting all they require in reaching their educational goals. Since Individual Education Plans are classified under special education the students with an IEP often requires additional assistance whether it is in the form of a scribe, or an Educational Assistant (E.A) to provide one-on-one help, additional time or use of assistive technology just to name a few which are all under the purview of special education. When an Individual Education Plan is created, for whatever reason, additional funds are granted to the school in order to supply students with what they require as per their Individual Education Plan. As like everything else when money is at stake it confuses and complicates things—people get greedy which leads to further problems like creating more IEPs than necessary. There is no doubt that school boards and schools need money to provide for its students in terms of teachers, books, technology and sporting events. Schools which are located in an area with people from diverse backgrounds the funding may not be the same as schools in wealthier areas; therefore, it is essential for some schools to get additional funding though various other ways and those ways are often through special education funding.

Students who are identified as learning disabled (L.D.), or Mild Intellectual Disability (M.I.D) require additional support for that student which requires funding to provide students with assistance from an educational assistant (E.A) or assistive technology and sometimes both. It is not to say that every learning disabled (L.D) student requires an E.A. sometimes it could be as simple as additional time to complete their work. It could also be simply providing a quiet area to work or preferential seating in the classroom. There are numerous different accommodations that could be listed in a student's Individual Education Plan. In this case, additional funding is not necessary. Nevertheless, many IEP's are indicating a need for assistive technology or additional support. In these cases, the school obtains additional funding because it is the law to provide whatever the IEP states a student requires in assisting him or her to reach their educational goals.

In the last few years there has been a big push lately for Assistive Technology by Ontario school boards. The advances in technological devices have made it more accessible in our schools resulting in many programs being created to provide assistance to students with learning difficulties. There are a number of programs such as Dragon Naturally Speaking and Word Q just to name a couple that help students with their reading difficulties. There are also voice recognition programs that will write out the words the student is speaking to assist him or her with their writing issues. From my experience as a high school teacher there is a big push for Assistive Technology (A.T) to provide the integral assistance for our special needs students. I have no issue with Assistive Technology facilitating students to improve their learning disabilities. However, instead of having smaller class sizes where the teacher or educational assistant can provide more support to students; school boards and the Ministry of Education would much rather spend money on programs that will do the work for the student as opposed to a person actually teaching our students to learn and be self-sufficient. We are training our youth to avoid doing anything for themselves because even in our schools we are enabling this behaviour to continue. By not teaching our students the fundamentals we are only teaching them to avoid independent work and independent thinking. It is a sad affair with the number of students who have difficulties reading and writing, but it is not surprising.

It is understandable that we live in an ever changing world where this fast paced technological existence encompasses our everyday lives. Regardless of the technology in our homes or in our schools we still need to know the basics of reading and writing. Just because technology can read and write for someone it does not mean we should forgo learning, and teaching such basics. A few years ago, the principal at the school where I was teaching sent out an email to the entire teaching staff regarding technology and its importance within our educational system. The question he posed, to his teachers, which garnered an abundance of heated dialogue, mainly from the English department, was his questioning if teaching cursive writing in elementary school was a total waste of time and effort because of where technology has gone over the last decade. Some people believe that cursive writing is on the way out because of technological devices such as iPads and apps associated with the device. Tamara Baluja wrote, "In the U.S., a majority of states have stopped teaching cursive writing in favour of basic typing skills" (Globe and Mail). It is ironic that some educational institutions are focusing on teaching students content they already know as in basic typing skills and forgo teaching content they lack as in hand-writing. The irony of not teaching students what they do not know in favour of teaching them what they already know. I guess that is the path to success teaching students what they already know as opposed to teaching them what they do not know as in hand-writing. There is no question that typing is more widely used than actual handwriting skills; however, the ability to write will always be needed. Even though technology plays a huge part in our daily lives, we still need to know the basics of writing, and yes cursive writing is still an essential part of our educational teaching or at least it should be. Many teachers were incensed that a principal would even ask that question. Will technology replace our need to sign our names? Will technology replace our need to ever have to read and write again? I sure hope not. That particular principal favours technology in the classroom as opposed to teaching the basics because he sees himself on the fringes of technological trends in education. He fancies himself as an innovator in educational trends with the hopes of advancing his own career ambitions or so it appears. When students cannot think for themselves no amount of technology will help with that. We need to teach our students the basics regardless of the amount of technology that shrouds our lives. Anne Mangen and Jean-Luc Velay argue that "handwriting of any kind plays a role in how the brain learns and remembers. Writing by hand, the researchers say, activates different parts of the brain, meaning the way we learn things may depend to some degree on how we write them down. So far Canada is sticking to the tradition" (Globe and Mail). Technology may be the present and future but without learning the basics of being able to read and write, how can we call ourselves an enlightened society?

Technology in the classroom can be beneficial in stimulating our students' minds as a way of differiented instruction; however, it should not be used exclusively in place of good old fashioned teaching. If it is always used then it becomes expected and then it loses all its cache. If teachers use technology too often it tends to lend itself as more of for entertainment purposes. Eventually students would lose interest forcing the teacher to find the next form of entertainment to get them interest. Technology that is used properly can be beneficial to differiented instruction for the special needs students. With all the technology around us it is understandable why so many children have attention issues (ADD, ADHD) because of all the images intended to grab our children's attention quickly which then leads to an avoidance of critical thinking skills. Our youth are losing their ability to think for themselves. Sometimes the tried and true is the way to go. The ability to read and write should be something our education system should strive for our students instead of just giving them programs to do it for them. The money spent on many of these "educational" programs could be spent on providing students with teachers and educational assistants to help our students succeed in their school lives and beyond.

As helpful as technological programs can be for our special educational students who possess Individual Education Plans it cannot, and should never take the place of face-to-face teaching. We need our students to take responsibility for their learning and to take pride in learning something for themselves. It goes back to my skateboarding analogy of learning to do something for the joy of it as opposed to having someone or something do it for them. In order to grasp something a person has to do it for themselves in order for it to be conducive to learning. However this ideology is not common within the special education departments because of the importance they place on assistive technology in our classrooms. It appears, in the minds of our education leaders, that A.T. is a far better resource for the success or failure of our students than actual trained teachers and education assistants. The irony is these same administrators made their bones in the classroom and now feel a more valuable resource for students is assistive technology as opposed to teachers and education assistants. Lucky for them their superiors did not feel the same way because if they did maybe they would not be where they are today.

Individual Education Plans can be extremely helpful for students to achieve their educational goals, but the recommendations should not be too broad. They need to be geared toward each student. In many instances, it is teachers who are given a resource period who are then expected to complete a student's Individual Education Plan. Often that same teacher rarely interacts or speaks with the actual student. They are given an assessment sheet and are expected to complete the recommendations with little to no training. What happens is the person adds certain recommendations like a student requires a scribe or quiet work area when they are not necessary for that particular student. These recommendations are added just to make it look good and to fill up the recommendation section of the Individual Education Plan. I can speak to the truth of the above statement as I was put into a situation where I spoke with the student for less than 20 minutes and was expected to complete an accurate Individual Education Plan based on very little knowledge of the student's educational needs. When the classroom teacher looks over the IEP and sees a scribe is required they end up photocopying notes for the student who likely can write on his or her own. When the recommendations in the IEP are not specific to each student it leads to a trend that enables students' lack of effort to continue throughout his or her academic years. By having this accommodation it leaves little in teaching the student to improve his or her writing because they rarely wrote themselves. When someone has difficulties with something the best way to overcome them is by doing it over and over. These particular students should be expected to write so they can improve the skill not avoid it and completely lose the ability to write. What does the adage say? "Use it or lose it" and so many students are losing it. As a result of wrong recommendations the student who never really had to write becomes a poor writer because he or she did not have to write all those years. I understand that some students have difficulties but the best way to overcome them is by helping them improve not remove them from learning the skill.

There are many students in this province that are identified who should not necessarily be identified and many others who should be but are not. If students were just pushed a little harder at an early age and were given the necessary help early on they could be achieving the success as expected. When it is absolutely necessary an IEP should be implemented; it just seems that so many students are identified simply because they have some issues early on that with some effort can easily be overcome.

A number of years ago I taught at a high school in Ontario and the first year I was hired there were just under 1000 students and after three years the numbers dropped to just over 800 students. Obviously enrollment throughout Ontario schools has declined and as a result many teachers were forced to become occasional teachers. Of the 800 students this school had there were nearly 250 formally identified students with an Individual Education Plan. This is a substantially large percentage of students with Individual Education Plans who require additional assistance in some form or another. Every IEP has certain requirements that each teacher must follow for every student in their class. Sometimes it is as simple as providing these students with extra time or providing them with a quiet area to complete quizzes or tests. Often times a teacher with an applied level class will have around twenty-four students of those it is likely that there are 8-10 students with IEP's. Along with preparing lessons the teachers has to keep in mind the recommendations for each Individual Education Plan his or her students have. Increased class sizes make instructional time more difficult and more difficult for the special education students to fully comprehend the content that is being taught. Otherwise, these students will only fall further behind increasing the chance of losing interest in the learning process. With that said students do not necessarily fall behind in the sense of having to repeat a grade because nowadays they are being dragged along whether they understand the content or are able to succeed within curriculum expectations. Consequently, they are falling behind in what they are learning because they are being pulled along their education careers. This is not the teacher's fault, nor does the blame fall entirely onto the principal's shoulders. This is a societal problem that needs to be looked at on the whole because in today's society we expect very little from our students because of this Oprahfication of society. We have permitted this perceived notion of being held hostage by our youth. We know it and they certainly know it. It is just simply easier to drag students along instead of just teaching them what they should be taught. Dragging them along avoids taking responsibility for teaching them and also avoids any chance of harming their self-esteem. The real world does not care about a person's self-esteem so by pulling or dragging a student only harms them in the long run because they do not know how to deal with adversity when they are faced with it. How will these students feel when they are thirty years old and lack the ability to properly read and write? I'm sure their self-esteem will be extremely low when that happens. Not only will their self-esteem and self worth be at a devastating low; government expenditures will be at a lamentable high because many students lack the ability to properly read and write. A large number of our youth will lack the ability to have careers; whereas, the government will be expected to provide for them financially. It can only be surmised that government expenditures will increase due to the "disability" payments that will be handed out. I hope the money the government saves now is properly invested because it will be needed in the future if a change to our educational policy is not done swiftly.

Dealing with adversity is vital to life skills which we should be teaching students how to cope with, and teach them about it at an early age. By allowing students to skate by on school work and their responsibilities only sets them up for failure. We often hear about the "real world" one major flaw we as educators fail to capitalize on is treating school like the real world; otherwise, we teach students that school is really not that important in their lives. Ontario students are being taught to avoid adversity which will be far more difficult for them when they have to deal with it when real adversity hits. A boss will not accept an employee who shows up late for work or who provides inadequate work especially during their probationary period. How will they feel when they get fired for something they were taught was acceptable behaviour throughout their school years? They will not know how to deal with getting fired because they have been taught to avoid adversity from people who should be doing everything to prepare them for their future. We have taught them that inadequate work is acceptable which is not how it is in the "real world."

Individual Education Plans are an exceptional asset for our special needs students; on the other hand, it should not be used or implemented for the sake of identifying a student simple because it is easy to do it. It should be used as it was intended—to help special needs students achieve their academic goals. In recent years, it has gone away from this purpose and simply an avenue to get students their high school credits. We need to teach them subject content as well as teaching them to be productive members of society—members of society who can deal with adversity when they are faced with it.

One final point regarding Individual Education Plans is the invaluable resource of education assistants. In an ever increasing need for additional support in our schools, EA's are a resource available for students who need them. Sadly, I have been in a school where it had nearly 250 students with Individual Education Plans with many requiring scribes or additional assistance. With that number of students with special needs it would be thought that the school would have plenty of education assistants on site. Consequently, that was not the case as many are not being properly utilized. For much of their time they were being misused by the head of the special education department. They were being devalued as a member of the school staff. Instead of having EA's work with students much of the time they were stuffing envelopes or running errands for the head of the special education department. Education assistants need to do the job they were trained and be treated like valuable members of the education system. They have a number of different tasks they are responsible for and very little time and support to do their jobs effectively. They cannot focus on a few students as they are being bounced around often doing tasks that do not benefit special needs students. They get little opportunity to build rapport with students as they are limited in a school so they go where the greatest need is at a particular moment-sometimes that need is not with the students' needs in mind.

The Drummond Report suggested a cut to support staff but it is obvious that Ontario's students need more assistance and not less as EA's are essential for Ontario's ever increasing special needs students. Instead of spending millions of dollars on programs that simply enable students that money should be spent on teachers and education assistants. Where the real value in the money spent can be achieved. It is ironic how the number of our students requires additional support is increasing because of an education system that has let them down, and yet this same education system is trying to cut funding for these same students. If we are not properly educating our children at a young age, and by this I mean providing adequate support to Ontario teachers, then these same students will require additional support to be successful, and added support requires funding—funding the government is trying to cut. The policy makers need to see what is going on, and how it is hampering Ontario's students.

Cell Phones in the Classroom

Today's high school students have been inundated with social media and the trend of communicating through text messages has exploded in the last number of years. It is a huge problem in classrooms trying to get students focused on instructional time and work instead of focusing on their phones. High school students cannot see how much their phones distract them and how much content they are missing because of it. Every single day in classes across this province, the battle over cell phones rages on and sadly teachers are losing the battle. We used to be able to confiscate the phones when they were becoming a problem; however, many parents were not getting behind the situation and complaining to school administrators and now teachers are not as likely to collect the phones if they disrupt the class. The image at the beginning of the book perfectly illustrates the paradigm shift of parents and teachers working together to now of a frequent butting of heads over issues. For the most part, children have trained their parents to buy into what they are selling even if common sense suggests that parents should be on board with teachers for the benefit of their children. In today's world, teenagers whine a lot about things not being fair and I guess many parents believe it is easier to cave then it is to stand their ground and listen to their teens complain. However this is why so many teens do it because they know it will work because they have trained their parents. It is essential that parents, teachers, and adults in general start showing children at an early age who is in charge and what is expected of them and what will not be tolerated. Parents want to provide for their children; they just have to do so even if their children do not necessarily like the outcome. Even though children like having the power over their parents they do strive under guidelines set out for them. Regardless how much children may want their freedom, they also want loving and caring adults in their lives. When a parent allows his or her child to have all the freedom they think they want they begin to question whether their parent truly love them or just wants them out of their hair.

For many families their way of communicating with their children is mainly through text messages. Providing teens with cell phones is largely how they interact with one another and is almost a necessity in today's world. The idea of eating a dinner together is almost non-existent. Time spent together is quickly being forgotten. We do not take advantage of family time anymore which is a shame. The time we lose as a family can never be reproduced later on in life. We are missing out of special opportunities to get to really know one another. We may all have technological devices that make communication easier but what it does is avoids that face-to-face interaction that is indispensable to the family unit. A family that communicates together sticks together.

On one hand, texting is a huge convenience because of the ease it is to communicate with each other. Although texting has proven to be a major problem in the classroom it is an even bigger issue within society. So many people are getting killed because of their inability to put their phones away while driving. I am sure the chiropractic profession will grow substantially because of neck problems due to constantly looking down at their phones while texting. How many people have, or know someone who has, walked into something because they could not take their eyes off their phones. Texting is not only consuming our teens. It is also consuming the majority of adults as well. Too many people think their phone is an extension of themselves and cannot give up their phones for even a few minutes. As HTC stated in one of their ads, "it is the last thing you see when you go to bed and the first thing you see when you wake up." It has become a huge addiction. The problem texting is causing in our schools, aside from being extremely distracting, is that it is leading to diminished spelling and grammar skills. Too many people claim that they have less and less time for what they feel as menial tasks such as proper writing. As a result, people are choosing to use short form in their text messages which leads to bad habits for teens when they write anything for school. Bad text messaging habits becomes hard to overcome because repetitive bad spelling leads to continued bad habits.

Look around and you will see the majority of people holding their phones in their hands, and this does not just apply to teenagers. Society has been acclimatized to social trends of texting, Facebook, and Twitter to name a few social networks. We as individuals as a whole cannot put down our smartphones even to eat so there is very little chance we will put it down to learn proper language skills. Look around the next time you are out for dinner at a restaurant and you will likely see people at a table with their phones next to their plates. This behaviour is a learned behaviour it has become socially acceptable in our society why would teens that have the tendency to follow the flock do otherwise? Teenagers are not programmed to be critical thinkers so therefore they follow what they perceive to be the norm. We need to teach children to think critically at a much younger age. Society is always placing a heightened importance on technological trends that we cannot help but follow. We used to say keeping up with the Jones' and now we have to keep up with the Jobs'. The problem is we need to work together—parents and teachers to overcome this massive problem of cell phones in the classrooms.

Lev Vygotsky (1896-1934) a well known psychologist argued that social interaction and culture has a dramatic impact on cognitive development. Vygotsky argued that cognitive process (language, thought and reasoning) develop through social interaction. That learning is conducted by social interaction of students using Zone of Proximal Development where students are guided by parents, teachers, and more knowledgeable people then themselves (ethicalpolitics). Vygotsky's arguments are even more viable today as it was when he was alive. Our individualized society has become less individualized in the last decade because of the globalization of communication through technological devices. It could be argued that since the beginning of time we have never really been an individualized society. Looking back at Greek and Roman periods people followed the masses. In ancient Roman times people flocked to the Coliseum to witness people fight to the death. The idea of watching brutality was a common occurrence because that was the norm. In the 1940s, the German masses followed

Hitler's law of eradicating Jewish people. I am sure many German people believed it was wrong but continued to follow because that was just what the masses did. We follow what others do because that is just the way things are and besides it is just easier to do so because less thinking is involved in following social trends.

For all intent and purposes today's society is inundated with social networks and global communication. Teens are no longer satisfied with a cell phone they need a Smartphone specifically the most up-to-date iPhone and they always need the latest technological device like an iPad to keep up with social trends. These new devices are excellent for developing globalizing network skills but are playing havoc with language skills. Proper spelling and grammar are becoming a lost art. Who needs to know how to write properly when technology can do it for you? That is a question that our students are answering with their diminished language skills.

The lack of language skills are not being helped by the current music selection that is dominating our air waves. I do not want to lay the entire blame on artists such as 50 cent, Snoop Dog or Eminem but the constant use of slang, vulgarity, and derogatory messages in their lyrics has dominated the language of our youth. When a person is limited to 140 characters he or she begins to use short form in order to communicate their ideas. The problem is it begins to take over within their everyday language and more importantly in their academics. Students are losing the ability to write.

We need to get back to teaching our students to write and write properly. Vygotsky believed that language developed from social interactions. We need to shape their understanding and knowledge and give them the freedom to illustrate that knowledge and expect the best from them and not accept mediocrity simply to asses and evaluate for the sake of doing so. Our students are losing the ability to write and then relying too much on spell checker to fix their errors; however, spell checker cannot fix everything, our students need to have the knowledge of simple words such as your and you're and there, their, and they're to mention a few grossly misused words—words that should be learned in elementary school. High school students should not, in any way, be making these mistakes nor should we as educators accept them. It is inconceivable that high school students "earn" their English credits regardless their academic level when they are making these types of mistakes in their writing. It does not look good on the individual school or the education system when its students are obtaining their English credits when they cannot properly use words that they should know by grade 6. It does not bode well for our educational system when these same students are going off to Canadian Colleges and Universities when their writing is far below what Canadian standards should be. This should be completely embarrassing to schools and the Ministry of Education when we are graduating students who cannot grasp how to use simple words.

Standardized Testing: Literacy Test and EQAO (Education Quality and Accountability Office)

In grades 3 and 6 Ontario students go through standardized testing to assess progress and comprehension of specific literacy and numeracy skills. The problem with these types of test is that it does nothing for the students but put added stress on them, and specifically added stress on the grades 3 and 6 teachers. I truly believe we need to challenge our students but to challenge them for their benefit—for their long term benefit and not to provide bureaucratic jobs that do nothing for the betterment of our educational system. When my son was entering grade 6 he was really worried about the test. He does extremely well in school and yet he was really concerned about these standardized tests. When I informed him that more pressure was on the classroom teacher and the school than the actual students he began to feel better about entering grade 6. The concepts of such tests are valid if the purpose of them is to make improvements in what is being taught and how it is being taught. It is believed that such tests are in place to stay on top of the best ways to improve teaching strategies and curriculum; and to evaluate how our students are doing compared to students from each school board and from across the province. This would be a valid tool if our education was improving over the years; however, it appears that our students are losing the intellectual battle versus students from stricter educational backgrounds.

Those, at times, valuable but often time wasting Professional Development Days should be used to enhance teaching strategies and to improve teaching our students how to be successful in learning and achieving true academic goals. Teaching literacy skills to our students should be done for the students benefit in mind and not for the schools. How and where a school ranks on the EQAO listing should not take precedent over the long term benefits of our future. Teaching literacy and numeracy skills should not only be done for standardized testing but to provide necessary skills to Ontario's students. Many classroom teachers teach literacy for the purpose of preparing the students to be successful on their EQAO tests because that is what is expected of them. Years ago, I interviewed for a grade 6 job and a question that I was asked was, "What was I going to do to ensure my students were successful on their EQAO tests?" I was not asked what I was going to do to ensure my students would be successful in their learning, just how I would ensure success for EQAO. Shouldn't the focus be on teaching our students life skills and to help them become lifelong learners instead of simply successful on the EQAO test? A greater importance should be on their lifelong learning as opposed to a standardized test. However with that said, one important question that needs to be raised is if literacy is a focus in grades 3 and 6 why is their writing so poor when they reach high school? It all goes back to the government's policy of lowered expectations from our students. There are so many high school students who lack basic literacy skills—the same skills that are pressed upon them in grade 3 and later in grade 6. As a result of the pressure placed on teachers to assist students to do well on EQAO they are obviously spending a fair amount of time teaching to the test. The concern is the appearance of the lack of importance on literacy skills after grade 6 because if literacy was important educators would not be constantly seeing the horrible writing that students are handing in and are permitted to hand in. The importance of literacy does not reappear until grade 10 for the Ontario Secondary School Literacy Test (OSSLT) which the students need to be successful in order to obtain their Ontario Secondary School Diploma. Has our education system simply become a tool for EQAO? Our students cannot graduate unless they pass the Ontario Secondary School Literacy test; however, they can graduate without doing much work throughout their high school years. Sadly, they can graduate misusing words like their, there and they're.

This in no way, shape or form places the entire blame on the classroom teachers. Teachers are constantly being scrutinized for what happens in their classroom, yet get very little support from administration and parents. When something goes wrong it is the teachers fault, and I am not afraid to say it that on occasion this may be true, but not always. When things go well the credit goes to the school's and the board's direction. What often occurs, in terms of literacy, is the student who have some difficulties is identified which require certain recommendations which normally involve some form of assistive technology. As opposed to helping those in need get actual assistance from either the classroom teacher or an educational assistant they are provided with programs that will do the work for them instead of helping them do the work themselves. As Vygotsky's ZPD (Zone of Proximal Development) clearly states, "to assist the student to learn by scaffolding the task or skill in order for the student to learn to do it on their own with little to no assistance" (simplypsychology). We need to ensure that the students who are using such programs are doing so to learn for themselves and not using the program to do the learning for them. The tools available could benefit many students, but only if used in conjunction with their own actual learning. We should be providing these programs to help them become comprehensive learners instead of relying on certain programs to do the work for them.

As was mentioned earlier, assistive technology can be a great tool to assist students to learn but not as a tool to do it for them—which is what is often taking place in Ontario's schools. We are not teaching students to learn, we are teaching students to find ways to have it done for them.

Classroom teachers have to deal with an ever growing amount of students who are having programs learn for them which makes teaching literacy even more difficult. Why learn to read and become a fluent reader when someone or something will do it for you? This is what learning in Ontario's schools has become and will continue to become if we do not put a stop to this atrophy of our educational system.

Somewhere between the grade 6 EQAO test and the literacy test in grade 10 there appears to be a slight disconnect in providing our students the necessary literacy skills to help them become lifelong learners. It is common knowledge that most boys do not enjoy reading. We are limited to a small group of students who still have a passion for literacy. What often takes place is the teacher conducts read alouds in order for all students to get some reading. We try to guide our readers by showing them proper ways to become fluent readers. Guiding them by giving them assistance they need to become independent readers on their own which goes back to the idea of scaffolding. We use scaffolding strategies to teach students how to become fluent readers on their own. Too many students are behind in their reading abilities because they may not have had that precious time reading when they were young. There are numerous different reasons why students have issues with literacy but becoming enablers is not the route our education system should take with our students. We need to be caring educators who provide the best for our students with their best interest in mind and not enabling their lack of own personal care for their educational needs.

It is mandatory that all Ontario high school students are successful in the grade 10 literacy test (OSSLT). The concept of making the literacy test important for our students is on one hand commendable because it expresses the Ministry of Education's stand that literacy is important. The way the OSSLT is conducted though shows a discernible disconnect between the perceived view of literacy and the actual view of literacy within Ontario's high schools. As it stands, the grade 10 literacy test is a complete waste of time and more importantly financial resources. Education Quality Accountability Office (EQAO) is just a bureaucratic organization that does little to aid in the improvement of our educational system and even less benefit for Ontario's students. All it does is make senior administrators pressure school principals who then pressure teachers, specifically grade 10 teachers, and anyone else involved in the literacy test to get results. The lead up to the test is extremely stressful because of the importance administrators place on this one three hour test. At times it appears the success of the Ontario Secondary School Literacy Test (OSSLT) is far more important to principals than the actual success of students' learning. The focus should shift from the literacy test to the lifelong learning of Ontario's students.

EQAO was established in 1996 as an arm's length agency of the provincial government to assist in improving the quality and accountability of Ontario's public education system by

-using results of province wide assessment to measure the quality of education in Ontario;

-leading Ontario's participation in natural and international assessment;

-reporting to the Ministry of Education, the education community and the general public; (EQAO).

This passage was taken directly from the EQAO website as a way to strengthen their importance in our education system in the minds of Ontario's leaders and Ontario's voters. The question and interpretation of how our education is improving, if at all, is left to one's own perspective. The bureaucrats have to believe what their agency is in charge of improving is actually doing some good for Ontario's students. If what the bureaucrats are doing with our education system is not proving beneficial then there is no need to keep the bureaucrats, and keep wasting our valuable resources on a failed agency. Ontario's Liberal government is cutting spending in order to bring down Ontario's deficit. It is good policy to curb wasteful spending so our children are not responsible to pay down our deficit. The talk leading up to the budget of 2012, especially after the recommendations made by Don Drummond in the Drummond Report is to cut spending by 15 billion dollars. Premier Dalton McGuinty requested this independent report to aid in moving Ontario, fiscally, in the right direction—sound policy for a responsible government for the people by the people. There was plenty of talk about a number of cuts to education by way of increasing class sizes, cutting all day kindergarten and cuts to support staff just to name a few recommendations in the Drummond Report. The obvious glaring omission for education cuts was that of EQAO and by that I mean there was no talk of cuts to EQAO. It is questionable why there was no mention of cutting funding to the Education Quality Accountability Office because there is plenty of money there that could be cut where it would not hinder the education of Ontario's students.

It was already mentioned how increasing class size would be detrimental to the success of Ontario's students and yet it was recommended as a way to cut spending. All day kindergarten has only recently begun being implemented in our schools. Support staff is a valuable resource to provide additional support to our students with special needs and to students who just need a little extra support to ensure their learning success. We are in the business of teaching students to be lifelong learners. The vast amount of cuts recommended in the Drummond Report do more harm to the success and improvement of our Ontario students. The cuts to education would directly affect our children and their education. Cutting teachers and support staff will only make learning far more difficult for many of Ontario's students. Sometimes money should not take precedent over what really matters—our children's education and their future. The bureacratics in charge of EQAO would have us believe they are making a difference in the improvement of Ontario's education system. Doctor Brian L. Desbiens, Chair of EQAO's Board of Directors states, "Monitoring how well these skills are being acquired is helping the education system deliver the best possible learning opportunities to all its students. Moreover, these skills can and should be reinforced in all subjects. Provincial testing has played a tremendous role as a catalyst for improving student learning throughout the province" (EQAO, Publications). The student learning improvement stated by EQAO is questionable because what needs to be discussed is what form of improvement is being done actual or virtual? These skills should be reinforced in all subjects but we must first stop allowing students to "earn" passing grades for mediocre, late and incomplete work.

On paper the bureaucrats at EQAO would have us believe that student improvement over the last decade is on the way up. Based on provincial testing numbers, from 2007-2011, the numbers illustrate similarities over this five year period. From 2002-2007 the numbers look even better as the success rate in 2002 was 72% and in 2007 it went up to 84% success.

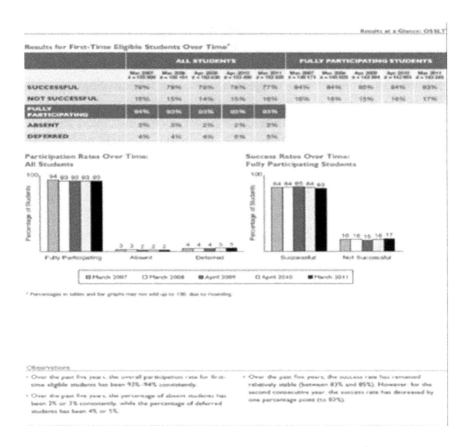

This can be viewed by going to EQAO's website among any other information you would like to look up.

From the students who participated in the Literacy test it shows the success rate in 2007 was 84%, with a high of 85% in 2009 and a low of 83% success rate in 2011. In the span of five years, the numbers have remained fairly constant which helps EQAO's statement that our students are getting the best instruction available to them. Nevertheless provincial testing has little to do with actual learning that Ontario students are acquiring. Others could look at the numbers and see a steady decline in student achievement on the literacy test. In 2009, student success was 85%, with 84% in 2010, with a further decline to 83% student success in 2011. The most recent OSSLT results have been updated and for this year the successful rate for first time writers dropped down to 82% which clearly illustrate a downward spiral for the last few years. Quickly looking at the numbers it is easy to come to the conclusion of a decline in student success because of the decline in the last four years. Since the numbers are so important to our "Education Premier" and senior administrators the numbers clearly illustrate that we are in a time of decline and something needs to change otherwise it will only get worse. We have to demand that our money stop being wasted by the bureaucrats at EQAO and use that money where it is needed—in properly educating our youth.

The number of deferred students has been higher the last two years over the previous three years. There are many different reasons for a school to defer students from writing the test, but the simple answer is numbers. Every principal wants their numbers as high as possible because that is what is expected of them and deferring a student who would likely not pass the test helps the school's numbers. There are different categories in terms of the test and the main category is First Time eligible students. The other category is previously eligible students which is not as important as the first category so deferring students whether they fail the next year does not hurt the numbers one way or the other. If students fail they have to take the literacy course (OSSLC) in grade 12; whereas, they need to pass in order to obtain their high school diploma. It is strongly believed the number of deferred students will be on the rise simply to boost the numbers.

To look at one particular school in Ontario we will focus on Parry Sound High School of the Near North District School Board. Parry Sound High School's numbers in 2011, clearly illustrate that this school deferred 7% of its first year eligible students. The reason for doing this was simply because these students were not expected to pass. It was Parry Sound High School's principal's first year in the position and he wanted the school's numbers to be at 82% or higher. Consequently, Parry Sound High School had a success rate of 75% for first year eligible students; far lower than expected by the principal, but on par with the entire board; which in itself, should be viewed as a success considering the demographics of the school. Nevertheless it was lower than the previous year when the school was under a different principal. As a result of wanting to better the numbers from the previous year, the principal had placed some pressure on the teacher who was in charge of the literacy test and all the training leading up to the test date. The particular teacher was pressured to defer more students than he did. It would have looked good as a new school administrator topping the numbers of that of the previous administrator. It was all about the numbers and the perception of having better leadership skills. It is hard to question his motives because of the pressure he is under to obtain the best possible numbers. It has a trickledown effect because of the importance on those numbers. Who is to say if I were principal I would not do the same? For that reason, I have no intention of ever become school administrator—too much politics involved. I want to be left alone to teach to the best of my ability and to inspire my students to set goals and reach for them. I expect a lot from my students and they know that because I do not expect mediocrity and they know I care about them.

The previous year, it was the principal's last year as she was heading into retirement and she wanted to go out with great numbers on the literacy test. She felt her legacy at Parry Sound High School as the school's principal would be best served if the numbers were great. Sadly, it appeared her focus was on the literacy test as opposed to the success of her students in terms of lifelong learning. It appears that in the minds of school administrators success on the literacy test automatically lends itself to success in life. That final test was her entire focus. She had only come to my classroom twice in two years, the first time was my first week to see what I was doing and the second time was the next year and only to tell me to focus my instructional time on teaching to the literacy test to my grade 10 locally developed English class. As I was a Long Term occasional teacher (LTO) I was doing just that and spending all my instructional time teaching to the literacy test. I believed that if I could get these students to pass it would go a long way in securing me future employment. Even though I was teaching to the test, I was doing so in a way that would help my students acquire the necessary skills to become independent learners.

In 2010, 11 of 198 Parry Sound High School students were exempted from the literacy test. Those 11 students amount to 6% of the students who were expected to write the test. Throughout the entire board at Near North District School Board there were 35 students exempted of which 11 of them were from Parry Sound High School. The 24 other exempted students came from the six other schools within the board which averages to four students per school while Parry Sound High School had eleven. These numbers clearly illustrate the importance that this school's administration placed on the literacy test. The province had an 84% success rate for first time eligible students, while Near North District School Board had 82% with Parry Sound High School having an 80% success rate. These are the numbers that count to senior administrators; however, it is easy to see how inaccurate they can be because of exempting and deferring students. It is all about the numbers and how each school is able to skew their numbers to improve their standing within their board. The real losers in the process are the students who are taken out of the equation of our educational system all so school administrators can be perceived as cutting edge in their leadership abilities. The true leaders are ones who look out for our students' educational benefit and not for their own professional agendas.

We will take a look at the numbers of Rainbow District School Board because it is within a similar geographic area of that of Near North District School Board and Parry Sound High School. In 2011, Rainbow District School Board had a success rate of 79% slightly higher than the neighbouring Near North District School Board's 75%. Lockerby Composite Secondary which is part of Rainbow District School Board had a success rate of 93% for first year eligible students. This same school had exempted no students while deferring only three, wherein the entire board deferred a total of 109 students. It is not a fair comparison between both schools because of the socio-economic difference between Parry Sound High School and Lockerby Composite Secondary. Parry Sound has a wide variety of students with varying economic backgrounds. There are a few haves and many more have nots in Parry Sound. Although it may not be a fair comparison, that is the case as schools look to other schools as a barrier to surpass. In the Rainbow board, I would assume that Lockerby would be the school other principal's aspire to reach and compare themselves to.

The Fraser Institute website of school ranking lists Parry Sound High School 462 of 718 Ontario schools; while Lockerby Composite

Secondary ranks 74 in the entire province. Once again it should be noted that comparing Parry Sound High School and Lockerby Composite Secondary may not be a fair assessment because of the socio-economic situation. The Fraser Institute states the average income of parents of students at Parry Sound High School in 2011 was $51,800 while at Lockerby Composite Secondary it was $87,900. The reason why I chose two schools that are obviously very different from one another is in relation to EQAO testing and how a school like Lockerby Composite Secondary will always fair better than a school like Parry Sound High School. The provincial test will always be skewed in favour of some schools over others just like in real life—sometimes life is not fair. The issue that needs to be addressed is how EQAO can make recommendations to the Ministry of Education in terms of curriculum. The Ministry of Education has their curriculum set for the province and not different areas of the province. There will always be some form of divide where recommendations made by EQAO based on provincial testing will not work. It is just the EQAO's board of directors' way to justify their comfortable jobs while our government makes cuts to real front line education workers.

There are conflicting reports about the cost of EQAO and each provincial test. There are reports indicating that the OSSLT costs the government over $15 million each year to conduct a test that really plays no importance in Ontario's education system.

Provincial assessments:

* Ontario:
Grade 3 and 6 (reading, writing and math)—$6 million each/yr
Grade 9 (math assessment)—$6 million/yr
Grade 10 (literacy test)—$15 million/yr
Cost or of running Education Quality Assessment Office (EQAO) which also administers TIMSS and SAIP—approx. $20 million/yr [6]

*Estimates of total cost vary from $50 million to $59 million each year [7] Provincial plans (currently on hold) call for more testing to be phased in to the point where there are exams in two core subjects per year from Grade 3 to Grade 11. [8] In June 2001, the Ontario Ministry of Education estimated that a new expanded testing program would cost $16 million annually, in addition to the $33 million already spent testing grades 3, 6, 9 and 10. Ontario directors have asked for a 3-year moratorium on the expansion of the current testing regime [9] (maritamoll).

The numbers vary between $32 million to $59 million dollars that Education Quality and Accountability Office costs Ontario's provincial government; more importantly, what it costs Ontario's taxpayers each year. This is astounding how much money is spent each year for something that does very little in improving education in this province. Just looking at the cost for the grade 10 literacy test each year could be spent more efficiently. That money could supply students with additional teachers, and support staff—the true areas for improving education in Ontario—not from standardized testing that simply does not work. It is completely mind-blowing how much our governmental leaders speak about cutting expenditures to bring down the provincial deficit and never hear any mention of cutting wasteful spending to EQAO—all we ever hear is cuts to teachers and support staff. These are frontline workers who entered the education field to make a difference, and yet these are the very people who constantly are under fire of losing their jobs. The fat cats at EQAO continue to get funded for something that most people in, and out of, education feel does nothing to improve the education in this province. We need to trim the fat that is clogging the arteries of the education system in Ontario.

Education Quality and Accountability Office began in 1996 and they continue to claim they have helped improve the education in Ontario. The board of directors will always go to the numbers in defense of their livelihood. They would claim the numbers speak for themselves in terms of improving curriculum that our students are receiving. They will argue that in the last decade the success rate has gone from 72% in 2002 to 83% in 2011. They will always go back to the stats as they would have us believe that stats do not lie. However, what the stats do not illustrate is the actual education our students are getting as a result of these standardized tests—something stats do not show. To quote the immortal Homer Simpson, "Oh, people can come up with statistics to prove anything. 14% of people know that." With that said, in the last two years the numbers have dropped from 85% to 83% success rate for first time eligible students. These numbers would indicate a substantial drop in the level of literacy education our students are obtaining. Any drop in literacy and numeracy is substantial and needs to be reversed before it becomes an even bigger issue. Instead of going to the numbers to determine if the education in this province is improving we could simply go to the source and find out that our students are not getting the same education as students did some twenty years ago. Ask any college or university professor if the education in Ontario's high schools are improving. The problem is not necessarily with the actual teaching that is going on but more to do with the ideology that students are no longer held to high expectation. Our students know that they can do very little and still obtain a passing grade. The issues are more of a social problem then what teachers are teaching. Our leaders need to make changes that will place a higher expectation on our youth to achieve higher standards.

In recent years, the grade 10 literacy test, and all EQAO tests for that matter has become more of a competition between schools and school boards to increase their numbers of successful students. It is all about the numbers. There have been a number of principals and teachers who have been caught and reported to the Ontario College of Teachers for cheating on the tests. Jennifer O'Brien of the London Free Press reported of a particular issue regarding a grade 3 math test. "The board has been investigating an allegation of cheating—by staff, not students—at Huron Heights French Immersion School on the 2009-2010 Grade 3 math test. Last school year, Huron Heights scored an average 77% in Grade 3 math, higher than the Ontario average of 71% and much higher than the Thames board average of 64%" (O'Brien). There are many other cases where school administrators have been caught for dishonesty on standardized tests. The pressure to be one of the top schools makes honest people do very dishonest things. There is a problem when provincial testing becomes an outlet where school administrators attempt to cement their leadership standing within the educational community. If this was anything other than EQAO, the Ministry of Education would scrap any educational tool that was not working, but for whatever reason it feels justified in keeping a failing program. The Ministry of Education will continue to waste money on a failing program over what truly works in the field of education—educators on the frontline working closely with Ontario's students.

One final point that will be made regarding the ineptitude of the Ontario Secondary School Literacy Test is that the Ministry of Education mandated that in order for Ontario students to obtain their Ontario Secondary School Diploma each student is required to pass the grade 10 literacy test. Ontario students must obtain 30 credits, complete 40 hours of volunteer, and pass the dreaded and wasteful literacy test. These are the guidelines and expectations set out for our Ontario students to earn their high school diploma. Setting forth expectations shows some education integrity and on the surface it is great policy. It clearly indicates substantial directives where it is black and white; however, in reality these educational expectations are filled with shades of grey.

In grade 10, students are expected to successfully complete the Ontario Secondary School Literacy Test. If by chance a student is not successful he or she receives another chance to pass the test the following year. Students who are unsuccessful in grade eleven are obligated to take the Ontario Secondary School Literacy Course in grade twelve. This amounts to simply showing up to class on occasion and doing a minimal amount of work to achieve a passing grade therefore fulfilling their expectation for their Ontario Secondary School Diploma. The question of educational integrity comes into light when it is said that literacy is an integral part of educating our students for lifelong benefit and yet a student can fail the literacy test at least once be put into a literacy course where very little is expected of students and yet still obtain their diploma. We are teaching our students that if they are not successful, for whatever reason, in time they will just be given some task with minimal amount of expectations placed on them to have some perceived educational integrity. Isn't that really what it boils down to having integrity within our educational system? When there is a lack of integrity it diminishes the entire educational process and devalues it within our daily lives. A devalued educational system does very little within the confines of our global placement in the world.

What the McGuinty government and the Ministry of Education need to do is do away with wasteful spending and eliminate EQAO from our "Education Premier's political mandate. It is the bureaucrats who are the only ones who are benefitted from standardized tests because surely it is not doing anything for Ontario's students. The money that the Education Quality Accountability Office is hemorrhaging from Ontario's taxpayers could be used where it would be best served—in our schools helping students who really need it. As it stands now, EQAO provides no educational benefit to the people who matter most—Ontario's students. The irony is that EQAO has yet to prove any education quality as it is obvious that our education is in trouble and in need of drastic change. It also lacks any accountability as those in charge continue to reap the benefits and continue to fill their bank accounts and yet pass the responsibility of failure onto others—onto the same people who are trying to educate our children and the same people who are continually facing cuts.

Writing: A Lost Art

Regardless of whether the Ministry of Education and senior administrators believe Education Quality and Accountability Office (EQAO) and specifically the grade 10 literacy test is helping Ontario's students the truth is literacy has declined over the last five years and it does not look to be improving. The ability to think critically has diminished the ability to write properly and is at a disheartening low as too many students rely on programs like spell checker to correct their mistakes. Others simply do not care that they misspell words. Far too many do not even care enough to reread their own work to ensure accuracy in their writing. The American poet and educator, Taylor Mali illustrates this point perfectly with his poem, "The the Impotence of Proofreading."

Has this ever happened to you? You work very horde on a paper for English clash and then you get a very glow raid (like a D or even a D=) and all because you are the word1s liverwurst spoiler. Proofreading your peppers is a matter of the utmost impotence. This is a problem that affects manly, manly students. I myself was such a bed spiller once upon a term that my English teacher in my sophomoric year. Mrs. Myth, said I would never get into a good colleague. And that1s all I wanted, just to get into a good colleague. Not just anal community colleague because I wouldn1t be happy at anal community colleague. I needed a place that would offer me intellectual simulation. I really need to be challenged, challenged dentally. I know this makes me sound like a stereo, but I really wanted to go to an ivory legal college. So I needed to improvement or gone would be my dream of going to Harvard, Jail, or Prison (in Prison, New Jersey). So I got myself a spell checker and figured I was on Sleazy Street. But there are several missed aches that a spell chukker can1t can1t catch catch. For instant, if you accidentally leave a word your spell exchequer won1t put it in you.

And God for billing purposes only you should have a serial problem with Tori Spelling you spell Chekhov might replace a word with on you had absolutely no detention of using. Because what do you want it to douch? It only does what you tell it to douche. You1re the one with your hand on the mouth going clit, clit, clit. It just goes to show you how embargo one careless clit of the mouth can be. Which remind me of this one time during my Junior Mint. The teacher read my entire paper on a Sale of Two Titties out loud to all of my assmates.I1m not joking, I1m totally ceral. It was the most humidifying experience of my life, being laughed at pubically. So do yourself a flavour and follow these two Pisces of advice: One: There is no prostitute for careful editing. And three: When it comes to proofreading, the red penis your friend (Mali).

Mali makes light of this lack of proofreading and lack of care for that matter that is constantly being submitted to teachers for evaluation. The bigger problem with spelling and grammar issues is the amount of students who simply do not care about taking pride in their work. Ontario students have been acclimatized to being apathetic towards their school work because that is what they have been "trained" to think. We have been accustomed to accepting mediocrity from our students and the more educators continue to allow this from our students the more it will happen. The quick and easy response to this dilemma is it is the individual teacher's responsibility to refuse to accept insufficient work from students. It becomes a classroom management issue in terms of elevated expectations. That is the quick answer to the problem; nonetheless, it is not the solution to the problem. It is like putting a band-aid over a bullet wound. The issue needs to be addressed in elementary school as well as by parents and school administrators by not allowing students to submit subpar school work; which again is the easy answer to the issue. It has more to do with not just the classroom teacher but with the entire ideology of our education system and for society for that matter. School administrators and parents must work with teachers to get students working on taking pride in their work. It needs to become habit forming so when students reach high school it is engrained in them to strive for high expectations, or at least strive for higher than base mediocrity. For the last couple of months I have been tutoring a grade 4 student, named Dayen, a couple of times a week.

I was informed prior to meeting him that he was reading at a grade 2 level and his parents wanted him to get extra help to improve his reading. I began reading short stories with him that were at the grade 2 level then moved up to the grade 4 level. I decided to speak with him about reading a chapter book so he could feel proud of his ability to read. After two sessions of reading the book he was excited to read and began reading more and more. His comprehension and decoding began to improve. He is showing great strides in his reading abilities. He has improved because of increased expectations and now has a sense of pride in his ability to read. We need to move our students, earlier on, away from the speaking in the vernacular, "good enough" mentality so it does not hinder their learning.

When students reach high school they have been accustomed to poor writing because of their reliance on programs to correct their mistakes for them. They lack the basic understanding of proper writing. This is not to say the entire blame rests on teachers because the Ministry of Education has said that students will not be held back regardless of their comprehension of subject content. Teachers will do what they can to help students progress but they cannot spend much time going over the same thing because of teachers expectations to get through curriculum. In the end, students will still move onto the next grade regardless of their understanding which is where the problem begins. Teachers will teach what they can and just move on while some students lack the comprehension to grasp further concepts later on. This is where we get into the issue with IEP's and also the complacency and apathy towards learning. The education system has done a great disservice to our youth by accepting their apathy towards learning proper literacy skills. If EQAO testing was proving beneficial for our students their writing abilities would not be so poor. Not only would they not be so poor, but it would not be getting worse from year-to-year. Students know that they cannot fail a grade in today's schools regardless how much school they miss and despite how little work they do—they know they will simply move onto the next grade. By teaching students that a laissez-faire approach will inevitably get them a passing grade just adds to the problem we are facing in today's classrooms. These same issues are now finding itself in colleges, universities and in the workforce.

The education system in Ontario is not necessarily broken, but there are many flaws and in desperate need of repair. We can no longer continue to waste valuable resources—our children. They are our future leaders, our future decision makers. Do we really want to leave this province into the hands of an apathetic generation of people who lack the skills to comprehend the English language? In order to fix the education system it has to be a collective effort where all stakeholders play a role in getting it back on track. Our youth will never buy into something if their role models do not first buy into it. Parents and teachers must collaborate together to help improve our students ability and desire to demand the best from themselves. It is also essential that school administrators support their teachers in what they expect from their students. The responsibility ladder must extend upwards with board administrators, Ministry of Education, and the current political party in charge of Ontario—at the moment that is the "Education Premier" of Dalton McGuinty's Liberal government. We need to remove political policy from the classroom and let teachers focus on what really matters and that is educating our children to be lifelong learners.

The Ministry of Education sets the curriculum and that should be their main focus but politics should remain with politicians and allow educators to teach our children to become positive members of society. Teachers need to be able to teach without any political arm's reaching into the classroom. When we get back to this ideology our students will reap the benefits.

As great as technology is, and can be, in our lives there is something to say about doing things the "old ways." Technology has made our lives easier at times it has made the world smaller. Technological advances has saved lives, but sometimes it has also diminished our ability to think for ourselves and in the grand scheme of educating our youth having the ability to think for oneself is a vital component to the learning process. Technology may have improved our viewing experience with our television sets; however, will these new televisions last as long as the old ones? Evidence is indicative that they will not—they do not have the power to survive. We have become a disposable society in terms of our technology—we should not do the same with our students. Technology should be used as a tool to assist our students in their writing, but it should not take the place of students doing the actual work. The ability to write should never be overlooked or taken a step back in favour of technology. There is still something to say about putting pen to paper and creating something for the pure enjoyment. Also writing with pen and paper will help students understand proper writing because they cannot rely on their spell check program to correct their mistakes as they write. Far too much emphasis is on the auto-correct program in our technological devices. Ironically, many people complain about the mistakes auto-correct is doing but still continue to rely on it. Our education is set up is to instantly give things to our students to make life easier; instead of teaching the basics and then using technology as an assistive tool to help them if needed. It could be used to reinforce what they are learning instead of just depending on technology right away. If students use pen and paper and learn how to properly generate ideas and develop them while accurately organizing these ideas grammatically correct along with correct spelling will benefit them substantially throughout their school years and beyond. As was mention earlier on, the physical act of writing with pen/pencil to paper aids in the cognitive development in our children. We need to continue to shape and develop the minds of our youth and using their fine motor skills will aid in their cognitive development.

Regardless how much students hate to take down notes it proves to be advantageous in cognitive development. Instead of succumbing to their animosity towards writing we should be enforcing more time for writing. By physically writing down notes it forces them to read the note, and then write it down giving them two options to understand and relate to the content. It also facilitates in grasping proper writing as they see how to spell words correctly as well as being kept apprize of proper sentence structure. By doing it over and over it will provide students with the proper tools to become effective writers. Having the ability and desire to write can be extremely cathartic while relieving some stress. This desire needs to be engrained in them at an early age. Once it is done early on, it becomes natural and not viewed as a chore and not faced with constant disdain.

The skill of writing should never be superseded by the skill of typing. Typing will always be there because of the amount of computers and smartphones that our children have access to everyday. These will be skills that students will learn on their own we do not need to spend a lot of time teaching them how to type. "When we give a student a task in the zone of actual development, the student can learn independently complete the task and there is nothing new to be learned, though such tasks may build confidence and fluency (some researchers believe that up to half of school time is spent teaching things that most of the kids already know and can do)" (Wilhelm 11). This could be a reason why so many students are disinterested in their education because they are bored learning content they already know. The skill that much of our students are lacking today is the ability to write. Having young students as early as kindergarten age writing will help develop their fine motor skills and give them pride that they can write their names as well as numbers. The ability to write will help them with their numeracy skills. Literacy and numeracy are the basics for all other subjects and therefore should be a priority to give our students the best chance to be successful throughout their school years.

Introducing students to journal writing for any number of reasons will be valuable as it helps them develop ways to express themselves. With all the bullying issues that plague our students learning how to express themselves through written language can be a way to communicate with teachers and parents what is going on in their lives. Sometimes children do not necessarily want to talk about serious issues like bullying to their parents or teachers; they may feel more comfortable subtlety informing parents and teachers of any issues that may be going on through journal writing. It could also be a good way to escape the confines of their inner struggles and find solace in their written words. Far too many students who are dealing with serious issues are afraid to speak out against their tormentors, whomever that might be—whether it is classmates, bullies, or members of their own family. They fear speaking out because being a "rat" may only cause bigger problems so they simply remain silent. That silence is why so many students resort to some of the things they do. Drugs, alcohol and suicide are ways students try to escape their demons when speaking to someone could ease their pain. When speaking is not a safe option for them they could turn to written format. We need to teach students a way to express themselves so they can communicate when something is troubling them and to help them overcome some of life's obstacles. A way of doing that is to show them journal writing can be helpful in so many ways. They can use a journal to express their feelings. It should be mentioned that journal writing is not the same as writing in a diary. Diary writing has often been associated, by boys, as something young girls do, and as a result they tend to shy away from journals because of their misconceptions of what journals are. We need to teach students at an early age that there are different reasons for journal writing. Expressing their feelings is only one form.

When students keep a continuous journal throughout the school year they can see how much they have improved; they can see if they have a particular theme in their writing. They will see how they are able to develop and organize their ideas. It will give them confidence to express their feelings and deepest thoughts in their journal. Through journal writing it gives them and outlet to write and improve their writing while possibly leading to a number of students finding a love of writing that lasts a lifetime. They will have the ability to organize their ideas, improve their spelling, receive feedback and refine and perfect sentence structure.

There are so many benefits in instilling writing as an everyday part of curriculum in all grades. "Writing is, by nature, personal and individual. In a world of peer pressure and sameness, from elementary grades through high school, writing can be a valuable way for students to nurture individuality and deal life's issues." Roy Peter Clark, teacher and journalist, says "that learning to write also means learning to think. The writing process gives students a path for clear thinking. Young writers must think independently and respond to criticism of their work." Instead of avoiding giving students constructive criticism because of the possibility of hurting their self-esteem we just allow their mediocrity to continue. "Writing is a solitary activity, and it results in something that belongs solely to the writer. It also helps the listening part of communication because a good writer listens to the teacher and writes down key words." Clark says, "Good writers also become good readers and speakers. A good writing teacher helps a student speak more effectively. The student finds her 'voice' on the page and shares it with others through oral interpretation; she learns to read her words aloud to others with feeling and emphasis" (Zinkosky). Even though technology is readily available in classrooms the art of writing must be continued to be used. As Vartan Gregorian, President of the Carnegie Corporation in New York states, "if students are to learn, they must write" (Zinkosky). Could there be a direct correlation between the lack of writing in schools with the diminished literacy skills that is taking place in our schools? We should bring back an emphasis on writing and maybe, just maybe, our students will begin to get something out of their education. Far too much emphasis is on technology and moving away from cursive writing. Technology is taking over, our students spend the majority of their time using technology in the classroom, mainly playing games, or checking Facebook, rather than using it for their education. There is such a push towards using technology or allowing technology in the classroom; simply to say that technology is being used even though much of the time it is being used as a time waster. Students are totally indifferent about their education and care more about the games on their technological devices than they do about their future. The short term goals of instant gratification of entertainment far outweigh any long term goals. As important as technology is in the everyday world Ontario's education leaders fail to understand that in most cases technology is not being used as they would like. We have a problem with the technological devices being used and until we start to realize that sometimes technology is not benefiting our students they will continue to get farther behind in their education. And farther behind on a clear understanding of what is expected of them in the classroom. It is becoming more frequent that technology is becoming a distraction for our students because they lack the ability to stay focused on the task at hand because of the technological distractions that dominate their attention. Our students are losing the ability to pay attention because a great number of them are easily distracted by the technology that our education leaders feel is necessary to have in the classroom. Attention Deficit Disorder in classrooms is growing and could be a possible link to the technology that our children are inundated with everyday. They are constantly being entertained with graphic images to keep their attention; otherwise, they quickly lose interest. The technological world is always moving; technology is always changing because that is what our society demands. That is why our education system is pushing technology in classrooms because of the entertainment factor, we as teachers are forced to play for our students. Our educators have to become more entertainers than teachers nowadays in order to hold onto our students' attention.

We have to continually come up with new and exciting gadgets to entertain as opposed to teach our students. Our classrooms need to be more education friendly and use technology sporadically in order to make the learning process much more geared to helping students get the necessary skills they will need to succeed in the future. That is not to say that technology is not important because it is in our world. What I am saying is we need to reinforce learning and use technology as an aid and not to entertain.

There are often arguments on using technology to make our lives easier. Why do mental addition when we could easily just use a calculator because the technology is there for our use. Just because a calculator will do the work for us it does not mean we should avoid teaching students the multiplication table or how to divide numbers without the use of technology. We need to teach the basics to our youth without always relying on a device to do the work for our students. We need to teach our students to think, we need to challenge them to rely and think for themselves—and by teaching, and expecting them to write will be the fresh start they need. This is no way suggests that a calculator should never be used to do math. I am only suggesting that we teach students the necessities of numeracy so they do not rely solely on technology. We want them to rely on their brains. I am sure we have all gone into a store to purchase something and the young teller at the cash register informs him or her how much change to give back. If the change is $9.96 and the customer gives the cashier a nickel it just confuses the cashier they have no clue what to do. In most cases, the customer has to tell the cashier how much change to give back. Yes, technology is there to ease our lives but we still need to educate our youth on the necessities of literacy and numeracy to avoid such embarrassing moments such as the one above.

By teaching students the importance of journal writing it will aid in their expressive writing. Ontario's students have the capability to express themselves; nevertheless, what they express may not always be appropriate, or a true indication of the individualized self but a reflection of the current trend within the confines of adolescence and that of social media. Teaching students how to express themselves in today's society of social media is important because of the constant bad behaviours by celebrities that our children look up to and try to emulate. We need to teach our students that expressing themselves, their true selves, is something they should not shy away from and something they should reflect within themselves and find their true identity. There are proven positive effects in teaching students expressive writing. Expressive writing helps students with "reduced depressive systems, improved working memory, higher students' grade point average, and altered social and linguistic behaviour" (Baikie and Wilhelm, Emotional). When students have the ability to express themselves they will have a far greater chance at dealing with difficult situations and then overcoming whatever they face. Our youth are constantly facing issues that cause them social difficulties whether it is bullying from other students, or issues at home they are inundated with events that lead our children to depression. Depression is taking too many of our students far too early in their lives because they lack coping abilities that something like expressive writing can help them deal with. Focusing on teaching students' expressive writing and expecting students to write expressively and to do the best of their ability may not save everyone, but if it saves one student faced with depression isn't it worth it? I will go in greater detail about depression and its effects on our students later on.

By enforcing higher expectations of our students in their writing and not accepting mediocre output from them will go a long way in seeing an improvement in our students' achievement. Setting higher standards for our students will help improve their working memory, their ability to think critically and be far better prepared once they complete high school. Getting 80s in high school is meaningless if they cannot write effectively, if they are not challenged and lack the ability to think for themselves. They go off to college, university and lack the ability to comprehend what is expected of them in terms of work habits, critical thinking and writing ability. The ability to write at an early age is the basis for our students to succeed in school and in life. Proper literacy and numeracy skills are essential in all subjects regardless if a student enters academia or the workforce.

This is no way says that schools are not teaching our students proper writing skills, it is just the education system tends to allow the output of mediocrity from our students as acceptable. The idea is just getting students to hand something in to be evaluated for the simple fact of evaluating students' work despite how good or bad their work is. On Near North District School Board's website it states, "We strive for excellence in education and continue to make significant difference in the lives and achievement of our students (NNDSB). It would be good if this statement were true because if it was we would not be so readily accepting of mediocrity from our students. Many of our students hand in work littered with spelling mistakes that could easily be corrected if they just took some pride in their work—which is often weeks past the due date. The work submitted can have pieces of paper torn, or splashed with food stains. Neatness for a lot of our students is not a priority, even when neatness generates a mark on the overall grade of the assignment. A total apathy is taking control over Ontario students and until school administrators refuse to allow it, teachers will have to continue to accept it. This all goes back to the numbers again. It could be easily said that teachers can refuse to accept such mediocrity and the problem would be fixed. This is easier said than done because if teachers started doing that they would hear it from their principals. The incident with the Alberta teacher Lynden Dorval is a perfect example. Principals want high success rate for students' achievement as in credits given out at year's end. The reason why principals want high success rate for credits given out is because their board administrators want earned credits to be higher. Board administrators want the number to be high because the Ministry of Education demands these numbers higher so the politicians can go to the voting public and say how well the education system is doing under their leadership. Teachers could refuse subpar work but then in the end they would just be pressured to bump up the marks to 50% anyways. It is an entire system problem that needs to be revamped for real change to take place within our education walls.

Ontario schools are teaching students to write journals and short stories. We need to continue teaching literacy, and stop accepting mediocrity just because teachers need to evaluate students in order to get them a passing grade and a high school credit. It does not matter how good the work is as long as something gets submitted. Short story writing has many benefits which is not to make published novelists out of all of our students. "They will learn how to concentrate and will be able to apply that focus on other tasks. Writing takes a lot of brain power. The imagination is given a good trashing and there are many ups and downs in the process of creating a work of art. They will learn to handle criticism, which hopefully is most constructive and positive, but the world is not always fair. Criticism is a very useful thing. Many people, adults included, take constructive criticism as a personal insult" (short stories). In terms of writing, constructive criticism the teacher provides in the work is far more important for the individual student than just the mark. Because the comments made by the teacher are intended to aid the student improve his or her work whether it is spelling, grammar or maybe sentence structure. For that reason I use to hide the mark within the comments so my students would have to read the comments to find their mark. It is pointless to add comments if students are not taking the time to read them to help improve their writing. "Their reading and vocabulary skills will improve dramatically. The interest will grow and the child will soon find the need to become more expressive through words. And finally, their confidence will be boosted when they have truly done remarkable work. If they are proud of their stories, they will be proud of themselves in writing and anything they set out to achieve. Individuals can't perform well outside until they are happy with themselves inside" (short stories). The educational system stopped holding children back because of the socialized issues of self-esteem problems that could occur. Although by just given our students a passing grade regardless what they do, or do not do, does more harm to their self-esteem than holding a student back a year. They then lack the necessary ability to progress to the next level which will inevitably lead to self-doubt. This only leads to a lack of focus and more disruptive behaviour as a defense mechanism to avoid being noticed for their lack of understanding and comprehension of subject content. In most cases, a student would much rather be labeled a "bad student" than a student who does not understand what is going on in class. Once a student gets to this point it will be extremely difficult to bring her or him back to the level they should be. This is where the problem lies with Ontario's students who lack the necessary skills and then they become complacent and apathetic towards their learning.

It cannot be said enough that students who are challenged and held to a set of high standards usually set out to achieve them. The problem in today's classrooms is the expectations set forth are simply so low that all they are expected to do is hand in something—anything—eventually and they will be successful. For years, this is what Ontario students have been taught and they are achieving the goals set out for them. "Latham and Kinne found, for example, that a logging crew assigned a specific and difficult goal were significantly more productive (and had better job attendance) than a similar crew who were merely urged to do their best (Peterson and Mar, 6). It would be nice if students did their best, but that is precisely what Latham and Kinne are stating that people who are told to do their best simply cannot quantify their best so they just do enough to get by. It becomes the responsibility of Ontario's educators, to not only set high standards, but expect these high standards to be achieved by our students. The adults need to be the adults and show our youth what is expected of them and that we will no longer accept their apathetic behaviour towards their education. Students look to adults for leadership and direction; they need structure regardless what they say and when we fail to do so, our children are left swimming in the mud. The leaders of our education system have done a great disservice to our youth. Our children need to see parents, teachers, and principals as positive role models who will show our children how they are expected to behave and to set limits for them. For the last number of years, we have lost the idea that adults are supposed to be in charge while our children follow. It has been a form of reversal of leadership because it appears the ones who are in control are the children and for whatever reason we continue to allow this to happen. It is almost to a point that adults are being held hostage by our children. The problem lately is we have been allowing our children to control us—to train us to what they think they want simply because adults want to avoid dealing with whinny children and teenage angst. However, the more we allow this to take place the more whinny the children will become and the more angst we will have to face in our schools and in our homes.

As it has been stated, the ability to write is an essential part of our students' daily lives. It does so much to assist them to improve their comprehension. It has also been argued that it help students improve their working memory. It helps our students express themselves with the written word and then through oral communication. It has also been argued that the ability to write has a cathartic feeling for students who are dealing with depression. The art of writing is such a valuable tool for our students we should be placing a greater emphasis on it in our curriculum, and doing so with high expectations. Throughout our entire lives we will have to write in some form or another regardless of our career aspirations so why not learn how to write properly and for a purpose.

In order to fix the problem, the Ministry of Education, board and school administrators, teachers and parents must make a point to enforce the importance of education to Ontario's youth. It should not be political rhetoric to obtain votes, not simply be a format for career promotions. The education system should be about educating our youth sans ulterior motives. We must stop allowing the behaviour of apathy to continue. Every stakeholder needs to take responsibility for the disarray in our educational system and in society for that matter. For the last few years, the behaviour that is taking place in our schools is a mirror effect of what is going on in society. Social media makes communication simpler, but it also plays havoc with our youth's desire to focus on their education. What is accepted behaviour in society should not be accepted in our schools and maybe it will be less acceptable within our society if we no longer allow it in our schools. When children enter school they should do so with the understanding that they must behave in a certain way. A way prescribed to them by the administration and teachers and supported by parents. This is the only way that these issues will improve. Maybe how our children act outside of school would improve as well. We complain all the time how the world is in bad shape and our teens have no direction or at least a positive direction. This is a learned behaviour; they learned that this type of behaviour is socially acceptable; it has been acceptable in our homes and in our schools because the people who should be leading them have failed. Now we have to right the wrong that has been going on in the last decade by taking back the power and showing our youth some discipline. I am not talking about punishment; I am taking about discipline. Our children need proper structure, they need discipline, and they need to know that their parents and teachers care enough about them to not allow them to ruin their life.

Just like everything else in life we go from one extreme to the next. In the old days, children could be slapped by a teacher or principal because of their behaviour, now we cannot say anything to students and they are taking advantage of it. In a recent story by CBC, it alludes to the behaviour of children going too far by making false allegations against teachers because they know they can get away with it. Professor Douglas Gosse states, "There's a general belief among many teachers that the pendulum has swung too far" (Gollom). We need to find a happy medium, where children are not being physically abused and where teachers are not being insulted, assaulted or falsely accused. There needs to be a mutual respect between both adults and children with the power and authority in the hands of adults. This is no way should be mistaken as educators becoming tyrants and going too far the other way, we need to find a middle ground of mutual respect. Our education system is not a democracy, but should be viewed as a form of oligarchy (less the tyranny) where the few rule and the majority follow the rules set out for them with their best interest in mind. As it stands now, schools are run as a mutiny as the students refuse to follow school and class rules and do as they wish because of the lack of consequences that they face. They live like so many of their favourite celebrities who do as they want without any real consequences. When there is little to no consequences there is really no reason to follow rules. It is the students who are the tyrants because teachers have little power to do anything because of this "Hug a Thug" mentality that precludes educators from doing anything. Students can show a total disrespect to teachers and yet there really are no consequences to their actions. Students will text in class, and even at times answer their phones in class and what are the ramifications?—NOTHING! The only thing a teacher can do is ask the students to put the phone away which usually does not get done. The teacher can send the student to the office where very little consequences will take place besides the threat of detention. Even if a detention is given out, students do not care because even if they do not go not much will happen but more empty threats of more detention time. This is where parents need to be onboard with the school and discipline issues. Oftentimes detention is not a deterrent because the student does not see it as a real consequence. So teachers do what they can to maintain some iota of classroom management without the appearance of losing face within the classroom. It is a battle that many teachers are losing.

Today's classrooms have become geared towards building self-esteem through group work. The majority of classrooms in Ontario have students working at tables of two or more to ease students in their ability to learn or so that is the intended thought. Consequently, students are losing the ability to work independently. They have been socialized to work in groups that they have lost the ability and desire to work and think independently. What often happens when students are expected to complete a written assignment either one person does it, or they waste most of their time and very little work gets done. "Many people find it difficult to write for many reasons. Even though there are many factors to consider, the skill of writing is a skill which can be learned. It just takes study and practice to develop writing skills. It is well accepted in both theory and practiced that the best way to learn to write is by doing the writing which is another powerful strategy that promotes discovery, comprehension and retention of information" (Inderwati and Hayati, 518). Working in groups is beneficial at times to collaborate with each other but working alone is also beneficial in supporting the ability to retain the skill of writing.

The Ministry of Education, school boards, and schools throughout the province should be embarrassed when students in university level high school courses, who plan on attending University cannot form a properly written sentence. What does it say when first year university students are having their papers returned because they are filled with spelling and grammar issues? When students enter university they should be prepared; university Professors should be focusing on the students' thesis and not spelling and sentence structure. Sadly, our university level students are not prepared for life after high school.

It is an entire breakdown of a system. There is such apathy within our students, and such frustration by teachers because of the lack of administrative support to really teach how they would like. Students work would be much better if expectations were just that—expectations because they are not being enforced within our education system. As it stands, students' expectations are much like yield signs, merely suggestions that most people rarely follow. Just like many laws that are on the books but are never enforced so why bother having them? Why waste taxpayer money by discussing and printing such laws. If it is important enough to make something a law then enforce it! Just like our educational system, if the Ministry is going to set student expectations in order to achieve a successful grade then it must be enforced. Students must reach these expectations or repeat the grade so they do attain the necessary knowledge and skill to progress to the next level in order to be successful in the future. There's a sort of Oprahfication going on with our educational system where the leaders of the education system in this province are like sheep following the social trend of what feels right as opposed to the betterment of our future through discipline and common sense. In a conversation with Dr Colleen Franklin, an Adjunct Professor at Laurentian University, she argues, "The thing is that everyone in a democracy has the responsibility to educate themselves on issues and express themselves and vote after they've done so. So many of us are refusing to be responsible." We need to take responsibility of the education system in Ontario, and make the appropriate changes for the common good for all our students, for our future, for the future of this province. If we do not stop this deterioration of our education system our children will be thrown into a sort of dark ages of knowledge with the risk of becoming a second or third world nation where Asia will be having us manufacture their good for simple dollars a day.

Our education needs a complete overhaul and it needs to begin sooner rather than later. We need to take a serious look at teaching writing skills early on and enforce high expectations from our students. The first change needs to start from the top and then move away from giving out grades and credits. We need to take a hard-line approach with our students and their education a sort of tough love. Our students know there is no credibility within the confines of our education system so there is a lack of respect for it. How can you respect something that has no credibility? In order for students to begin respecting their education, the people in charge of it must respect it as well. Respect it enough to care about making the necessary changes.

The writing abilities from Ontario's university level students are at a disheartening low. Dr Franklin states, "We can't count on them being able to write a decent essay when they arrive." These same students are leaving high school university level classes likely with a minimum of 80% or higher because they did get accepted in university, and yet there are disastrous issues with their writing skills. The problem is the lack of expectations placed on high school students. When students submit their homework—only a week late—they will likely get at least 70% regardless of the content of their assignment because oftentimes work is much later than a week. An assignment that is only a week past its due date is almost shocking to teachers. High school students are not being prepared for university. Dr Cameron McFarland, a Nipissing University Professor, stated that he was, "perfectly happy to teach students how to research and theorize and even how to write a university—style essay (as opposed to the dreaded three paragraph essay), but wants students to be able to write a grammatically correct sentence and understand what a paragraph is. It is a pleasant surprise—even a relief—to find even one good writer in a class these days" (Franklin). This should be extremely embarrassing to our government and senior administrators, to hear what is going on right now in our schools.

A problem that needs to be brought to light is the number of teachers who simply have lost the passion they once had because of all these societal issues that have entered the classroom. Most teachers enter the profession because they want to make a difference and yet these issues have turned many away from the profession. They have been jaded because of the lack of support that has gone on in the last decade or so that they just go through the motions. If students do not care, if parents do not care, if principals, senior administrators and the Ministry of Education do not care why should the teacher? Many older teachers become frustrated that all the work they do is all for naught so they to become complacent causing a breakdown of the system. A lot of older teachers just do not care and who can blame them? "They can't be bothered to hold the kids' feet to the fire about these issues. Frankly, I hear that more and more from my colleagues, as well as—I don't have time to correct their spelling and grammar—as long as I can figure out what the thesis is, I give them a passing grade" (Franklin). I once had a poster in my class that read, "I don't give out marks, you earn them." We need to get back to that ideology of having students earn their marks as opposed to just 'giving' them out so students pass. We are not doing our job if we continue to accept less than what is expected from university level high school students. By doing so we are making a mockery of the education in Ontario. Many students are leaving with a university level high school English credit and yet fail to understand proper sentence structure or even proper spelling. If a high school student cannot decipher when to use (their, there, they're) they should <u>never</u> 'earn' a grade 11 and 12 university level English credit in Ontario.

The technological approach in classrooms has become a contentious issue at times because of how it is being used and used as a time waster, and disruptor than used for good. The lack of interest in their education has been engrained in them at a young age and continues even in university. Dr Franklin mentions, "In the last few years I have had students coming into my office sulking and arguing that they've given me a paper and they don't see why they have to redo it (it used to be that students were actually very grateful for the direction and help). They talk, text, FB, and play games in class; one hates to banish the laptop, as some students actually use theirs to take notes. They are late to class; they skip class constantly; they don't prepare for class; they leave class early. It is like teaching grade school to teach university these days. The two greatest problems that I see in students coming into the university system these days are 1) a lack of academic preparation and 2) a lack of discipline" (Franklin). We need to take a step back and make changes to how we educate Ontario's students because it is obvious we are not on the right track and it will not repair itself.

Communication Breakdown

There needs to be some form of communication between our different levels of education in this province because there is a great divide between high school and college or university. Professional development days at the high school level is often wasteful as very little professional development takes place. All it does is give students a day off. What should be considered for a development day for secondary school is some form communication where the local university sends a few of their professors to discuss with high school teachers what is going on at the next level. It does not necessarily have to be in person as many high schools are outside of a college or university. It could all be done via video conference call. Schools do have all this technology at their disposal; it could be used to implement change at very little cost to the actual school boards. There is a push for students to use technology in Ontario schools it could also be used for educators to educate each other. The costs would be much lower than they are now and more effective professional development would take place. It could also be geared towards specific subject content and what is expected and what is being produced at the post-secondary level. This can also work with members of the community by bringing them in to discuss what they are seeing in the workforce. If we all come together it could make for positive change. It could actually become a truly professional development day where teachers are developed professionally It would not be that difficult to get going because I am sure college and university professors would be willing to take part in a professional development day with high school teachers. Whether it is in person or via videoconference it would help make their lives easier when high school students get to them. By opening up the doors of communication between secondary and post-secondary educators it would help in how to better educate students in what will be expected of them later on. Teaching at the secondary and the post-secondary level should not be mutually exclusive.

This Oprahfication of our society of doing whatever makes you feel good comes at the expense of our education system. It is also causing our students to only do things that grant them instant gratification and thinking critically about their education does not do that—so they don't. It does not help that our children are witness to the social glorification of complete wastes such as the Kardashians and those individuals of Jersey Shore. I cannot fathom the idea how the media and the entertainment business can glorify people like the Kardashians, Snooki and the Situation by providing them any facet of fame within our entertainment world. Our education system is facing financial cuts because of economic issues, and yet these individuals who lack any moral fiber, any form of integrity, or global importance have millions of dollars thrown at them for essentially being complete ignoramus' and symbols of what is wrong with our society.

The issue with our education system is everyone follows everyone else. It is analogous to a flock of sheep going around in circles following each other with no discernible leader. Somewhere, somehow we need a dog to get the sheep in line and bring them along for the journey to a destination of higher learning. At the moment, the education system in Ontario is lacking a dog. Dr. John Izzo argues, "We humans are social being, and fitting in matter to us. Human behaviour is contagious, good and bad. Responsibility is contagious. When someone steps up to change things, others step up, and find courage they had not previously found" (Stepping Up, 10). At present, there has not been anyone in charge, who has stepped up to right this ship which is sailing off course. The education leaders in Ontario have failed to notice the iceberg right in front of us. I do not intend to sound a tad pugnacious in my discourse about our educational system however it needs to change and it needs to change now!

Disenchantment of Real Life

I remember when I was a student-teacher and I took part in an in-school departmental meeting regarding certain directions some schools boards were taking regarding student achievement. The principal, at this particular high school where I was doing my placement, spoke about one school board in Southern Ontario and their approach towards students' achievement. Even as an inexperienced student-teacher, I was floored when the principal inform us what was going on. I believe he was thinking about incorporating the ideas in his school and wanted to gauge the reaction from the handful of teachers that were there. Seeing how I was only a student-teacher I did not say anything to the principal for fear of any possible consequences and plus I did not feel it was my place to speak up. However, I did express my concern to a couple of teachers who were in attendance, after the principal stepped out of course. The issue that was brought up was student achievement and the direction of how teachers evaluate students' progress. The idea was valid and worthy of discussion, but the way of evaluation was totally counterproductive to real life. It was all about the numbers and that was it. The principal mentioned that how can we evaluate students' comprehension if they have not submit any work? The quick retort was we cannot give them a mark if they do not submit any work. They would get a zero mark. If a student does not do the work they cannot receive a mark pure common sense or so I thought being a student-teacher. The issue that was brought forth was that a student who has not submitted his or her assignment for evaluation has not proven that he or she cannot do the work, or does not comprehend the content just that they failed to submit their assignment. The general theme was students who refuse to submit their work for evaluation should automatically get 50% because, as the argument goes, he or she did not show the teacher that he or she cannot do the work, or does not understand the content, just that they did not do it. When and if, the student submits their work then their mark can be improved from the base 50%. Of course this idea of 'giving' students 50% for not doing their work was completely vexing to me, and I was only a student-teacher at the time. I could only imagine how disturbing it was for veteran teachers. I was speaking with another teacher, and asked if that applied in the real world? Of course I was being sarcastic. So, if you do not show up for work will you still receive half your pay? That comment generated further discourse on the issue. When the principal returned a teacher brought up the same question I had posed moments earlier. Of course the principal laughed and responded with a firm negative. For the next thirty minutes some professional banter took place regarding if such a policy was implemented it would do nothing but further set students up for failure. Students would realize that even if they do nothing they would 'get' 50% which is a passing grade so why would they do any work? In essence students would be taught that doing no work in school is perfectly fine and acceptable. How would this benefit our youth? They would go off in the world believing this behaviour was not only acceptable, but expected. They would go into the workforce with absolutely no work ethic leading to serious issues when they are unable to hold onto a job. What will this do to their self-esteem?

It is absolutely inconceivable how granting students' minimum 50% for not doing any work is something that would be perceived as beneficial to students. The only thing this ideology does is improve the school's number of granting credits. How is teaching students that doing nothing will still get them a passing grade? They will still be successful regardless of their lack of work and lack of effort? This is a very slippery slope and it is incomprehensible to even suggest that this type of policy take place let alone actually going through with it. It is bordering on disgusting how much the education system is letting down our students and letting down our future. This has far more to do with politics and making graduate numbers look much better than they really are. The policy of permitting children to do little work and still be successful in school is a wide spread policy that is harming our education system, more importantly harming our children's future. I am sure the individuals in charge of our education system understand the ramifications of what is going on, but are taken in by what others are doing simply to get the numbers they need in order to compete with other schools. It is essentially follow the leader, the problem the "leaders" are not leading by example. Dr John Izzo mentions a story that fits perfectly with what is going on in Ontario's education. "Researchers filled a movie theatre with participants and projected a small light on the front wall. The study participants were told to raise their hand any time they saw the light move. Several confederates—that is, research team members posing as participants—also sat in the theatre. After about ten minutes one confederate raised his hand indicating that he had seen the light move. A minute later, another confederate raised their hands to say they had seen the light move. By the end of the study, most participants had said the light had moved, even though the light never moved. Our human tendency to follow the behaviour of others is deeply engrained. This tendency has negative consequences when groups of people act together as a riotous mob. But this trait also means that when we choose to step up to create positive change chances are very good that we will start a chain whose end we cannot ascertain" (15). It is obvious there is a negative aspect of what is going on in the education system and which is being followed by the masses. It is time someone steps up and takes responsibility for making changes, necessary changes for the betterment of our future. There have been many people who have written about the problems within our system hopefully our voices begin to be heard.

When a school has high graduation numbers it looks good for their board, to the Ministry of Education and it does not matter how schools obtain these numbers just that they do. Because when the graduation rates are high the provincial government can boast how well the education in the province is doing at that particular time. It is not about the future, it is about right now because an election is never too far off and it is all about the perceptibility of our education and not on any realism of the state of our education. The entire system is set up for short term goals because the elected government has a limited amount of time to hold office. They do not think about the next decade they think about today and tomorrow which leads to problems we have been facing for the last decade or so. Large portions of the voting public often go to the polls misinformed and base their decision on misinformation. The populace knows our education system has serious issues and is in need of repair; however when our "Education Premier" Dalton McGuinty proudly tells us that we have an 81% graduation rate then we feel good about the direction of our education system and what the government is doing. How Ontario gets 81% is not important to our leaders as long as we get there. Really that is how school boards function; they really do not care how schools get the numbers as long as they get the numbers. Our leaders bury their heads in the sand when it comes to how the numbers are achieved, as long as they are achieved. How these policies affect our students is merely an afterthought because what truly matters in the grand scheme of things are the numbers.

Getting the Numbers

Our education is a numbers game as these numbers are extremely important to school and board administration because at the end of the year that is how school and school boards are judged—based on their numbers. The amount of students who 'earn' their credits, and how many students graduate is the proverbial bar in which our education is quantified. The level of education and what they acquire when they leave their institution of learning is irrelevant as long as the numbers illustrate a level of achievement that can be expressed as a success rate for our governmental leaders. It is all about what is perceived of what our students are getting from their four years in Ontario high schools. As long as there is some modicum of achievement on the part of our students once they graduate with an Ontario Secondary School Diploma. The numbers are important and it should not be interpreted that I do not believe there is no value in obtaining the numbers—the point that I am trying to make is the numbers should not be more important than the education our students are obtaining. An Ontario Secondary School Diploma is worthless if our students are not prepared for life after high school. We need to put real value in that high school diploma. It should not just be given away. It needs to be earned. Let's make an Ontario Secondary School Diploma a valuable piece of paper where our students take pride in receiving. The ability to breath should not be the sole expectation in obtaining an Ontario Secondary School Diploma.

There is no doubt in anyone's mind that things are very different in today's age then it was fifty, or even twenty-five years ago. Back twenty-five years ago there were still possibilities of obtaining a good job. Fifty years ago there were a plethora of good paying jobs for those without a high school diploma. Things were extremely different then and for some people school was not very important because of the opportunities that were there for them. Twenty-five years ago a high school graduate still had opportunities to make a substantial living to provide for themselves and their family. Tradespeople who had the proper skills could join the workforce right out of high school and make a career out of it. There was more of a push to get accepted into a university to obtain a good career as was the common rhetoric. Consequently, in today's global market a high school diploma is only seen as important because it is essential to get into a college or university. Even with a university degree or a college diploma it is difficult to obtain and hold onto a job for any length of time let alone until retirement. The days of staying in one job for thirty years are almost non-existent today and that is with a post-secondary education. The world is ever changing and we need to be prepared, skilled and flexible when changes arise that will throw our lives in a quandary of uncertainty. In order to do so we need to properly prepare Ontario's youth how to cope with uncertainty, that will surely take hold of their lives at some point. This is why enforcing a value system into a high school diploma is vital for the future of the people of this province.

It is already well known that there is very little chance at a successful career with only a high school diploma and even less without. Nevertheless, it is also common knowledge that there is little value in a high school diploma because of the ease in which it is to obtain one. It was already mentioned how some school administrators conduct their school activities to increase the number of credits their school gives out each year. There always has to be some tangible improvement from one year to the next. There can never be a drop otherwise it looks bad on the school and the principal and no principal wants that because it would hurt his or her chance at furthering his or her own career within the educational ranks.

A few decades ago if a student did not earn 60% in elementary school he or she would have to either repeat the grade or attend summer school and many students did in fact do that. It made them work so they did not have to repeat a grade; they learned that if you do nothing, you get nothing. It may not have been perfect because some feelings were hurt and some students were upset that they either had to go to summer school or repeat a grade. However it taught them that if they were not able to do the work or if they did not do the work there would be consequences. By allowing a child who cannot grasp particular subject content to move on will only make learning more difficult for that student. Sometimes taking one step back to take two steps forward is needed. What we have now is a bunch of children with a sense of entitlement that whatever they do, or do not do, there is no consequence. However, most actions have some consequences whether we see it or not. The consequences that our children our going to have to confront because of this Oprahfication of our education system is a total letdown of our place on the global stage. We are setting up our youth for failure, a catastrophic failure of a few generations of Ontario's children. We are all to blame for continuing to allow this mismanagement of our education system. We are playing Russian roulette with our future. There are only so many Wal-Mart jobs out there. Not that there is anything wrong with Wal-Mart jobs.

In high school, students were expected to obtain 50% in order to earn a passing grade, if not the options was either spend some time in summer school or repeat the class. Again it instilled some form of responsibility from the student because there was little sympathy for students who did not attend class, or who did not reach the necessary goals. Maybe if a student ended up getting a 49% the teacher could bump up the mark to 50% if the student was deserving of some sympathy and compassion but again this was usually based on the individual student and if the teacher felt the student deserved the extra percent. Unfortunately, this way of thinking is far different in today's schools.

I remember receiving an email back in June 2009, from the principal reminding all the teachers that students who achieve between 46-49% on their final mark must be bumped up to 50% so the student can 'earn' his or her high school credit. A 50% on a report card represents that the student needed the teacher to bump them up and when 51% appears it usually indicates the student finished with 50% but that it was a legitimate passing mark as opposed to a bump up. This way that particular student's future teachers will know it was a real pass when they go through the student's Ontario Student Record (OSR). I have no problem adding a few marks to help a deserving student who truly did his or her work, but had some difficulties with a test or exam because some students may understand the content, but not test well. The last month of the semester, I would tally up every student's mark and have a one-on-one conference to discuss certain issues and what needed to get done in order to increase a mark. They had the option to redo an assignment or test so it was the student who had to take responsibility for his or her success or failure. Sadly, in reality, a very low percentage of students would actually take me up on this offer because they were aware of how things work and that they would get their credits regardless. Back in 2009, the bar was set at 46% to bump up to 50%. It was a stretch but each case is different and maybe a 46% was deserving of an increase to 50%. I truly believe the idea can work as long as the student does not know what took place, and they believe they truly earned the 50%. Once they find out they got bumped the evaluation process loses its credibility. In June 2011, I was called down to speak with the principal, it should be noted it was his first year as a school principal; the reason for the discussion was student achievement. I was not the only teacher called down to speak with him as many of us were summoned down to his lair of authoritative dominance. Throughout the year he used intimidation tactics to get his point across to his teachers. It did not matter if it was a new teacher or one who was there for twenty years he spoke with an air of superiority and what he wanted he got; he left little room for professional discourse between he and his teachers. So when he called me down to discuss a particular student, I had in a grade 10 academic course I had little say in what was going to happen. This particular student did very little work and the work that was submitted was not at the academic level. This student ended up with 41% at the end of the year, which was the reason for the call down to meet with the principal. As soon as I entered the room the principal was all business and brought up this particular student and "asked" me if I was comfortable with bumping this student to 50%. In truth, I was not comfortable doing it because if I did I would have done it before I submitted my marks to the office. I would like to mention that at the time I was a Long Term Occasional (LTO) teacher which means at the end of the school year I would have to start looking for work again. I had a year-to-year contract which is stressful because of the constant unknown. So, as a Long Term Occasional teacher I was hoping to get hired on for the following year. I said what the principal wanted to hear and that I was comfortable with having this particular student 'earn' his credit. I did mention that I felt it would be best if this student would be put into the college level course in grade 11 as opposed to the university level. He said he could accept that and then I left with my proverbial tail between my legs and my educational integrity left in the wake as the student was bumped from 41% to 50%. In two years, the bar went from 46% to an amazingly low 41% for student achievement. Who is to say other teachers with students lower than 41% were not 'asked' the same thing. This all goes back to numbers as being a first year principal he wanted the numbers to increase over the previous years' school administration to shine a light on his leadership abilities. My concern with this ideology is when will it end? What will be the number 35% or as low as 32% to pass how far will principals go to get the numbers they want? Or will it be the minimum 50% regardless of the work. Will it come to the bare minimum to 50% to all students before they even hand anything in to the teacher? As a university professor once wrote to the Globe and Mail, "I hope I am dead before these students run the country."

The evaluation process for secondary school students is so grey that students are always given the benefit of the doubt. It is a surprise that not all students 'earn' their credits in today's age. Many principals are continually encouraging teachers to bump up students' marks. A teacher can use his or her professional judgment and choose not to count any number of evaluations for any particular student so his or her marks reflect a passing grade. Many teachers are frustrated with the process of students getting bumped up to 50% by the principal, so teachers just give out marks. If the education system does not care, why should the teacher? Why should the teacher add stress to his or her life when it appears that nobody else seems to care?

Evaluation and Assessment are essential in having some form of bar where the education system can gauge our students' progress. We always need to strive for improvement because without any improvement it becomes stagnant, and a stagnant education system is bad as one that does not care about our students' future. The Ontario government is committed to enabling all students to reach their potential, and to succeed sounds great but it should be more than just written in a document, it needs to be implemented for the benefit of all our students. The money spent on creating a document expressing the government's educational direction is a complete waste of money when all it does is put on paper some ideas of where our education is going and how the government plans to get there. It is meaningless if the discourse of the educational direction is opposite to what is actually going on in our Ontario schools. All it does is make the government look good in print form when it reality the education system and the process of evaluation is in a complete downward spiral. "The present document updates, clarifies, coordinates, and consolidates the various aspects of the policy, with the aim of maintaining high standards, improving student learning, and benefiting students, parents, and teachers in elementary and secondary school across the province" (Growing Success,2). The document clearly states how our students are to be evaluated for their success and to reach their potential, but in reality and what is going on in schools is totally different from what is suggested in these documents. We all know what we want in terms of how our students are learning and learning for their benefit but the outcome is far off the mark.

The Growing Success document goes on to state that, "students and parents need to know that evaluations are based on evidence of student learning and that there is consistency in the way grades are assigned across school and boards throughout the province. With this knowledge, students can have confidence in the information they use to make decisions about secondary pathways and post-secondary opportunities" (2). This all sounds great on paper; however, as it has been expressed a number of times already this is no way illustrates the reality of what is going on in our schools. What needs to be done is getting down to the real issues that take place in our schools and if it means to take a step back, then we need to take a step back in order to improve on the current situation. We need to get to the root of the problem and stop masking our issues with political rhetoric which totally ignores the issues because ignoring them means we do not have to admit there are issues. "The primary purpose of assessment and evaluation is to improve student learning" (Growing Success, 6). It seems so obvious because that is the way to gauge how much students are learning, and where they need extra assistance. Teachers assess and evaluate student learning all the time, but when students are not showing any learning or displaying any output they cannot be assessed, nor evaluated. If they cannot be evaluated they should not be given a free ride because that in no way prepares them for the future. It does far more harm than good. Our education system in Ontario needs to be an innovator and totally rebuild this broken system for the betterment of our students, for the betterment of our future in Ontario. Let Ontario make the change first and others will follow.

I am sure you have seen the learning skills portion of a report card. Every student in Ontario from grades 1 through 12 is evaluated on their learning skills. If reported properly this can provide parents with a far better picture of their child's progression than just a numeric value. But again learning skills must be evaluated properly for it to be an effective tool in assessing and evaluating Ontario students.

A few years ago, the principal at the school where I worked was adamant that the learning skills be on par with the students' actual grade. There are plenty of students who can achieve 80% in their class, but show absolutely no initiative or responsibility which should garner them either an "N" (needs improvement) or "S" for (satisfactory); however, this one particular principal expected students who obtained 80% or higher to have all "E" (excellent) on all their learning skills. Also, a student who obtains a 59% or lower should get all "S" or "N" on their learning skills because learning skills should be a direct correlation to their final grade. There are plenty of students who do their work, they hand in assignments on time, are responsible for their behaviour and who approach new tasks with a positive attitude, yet still earn 50s and 60s in their classes. These students should not get needs improvement or satisfactory simply because they get 50s because their actual learning skills would be high. On the other hand there are students who never submit work on time, who constantly do not use their class time wisely, and always have a negative attitude, but can pull off 80s in their classes—should these students get all excellent in their learning skills? A student can earn 80s and yet deserve a *needs improvement* in certain learning skills. If we are going to place an importance on learning skills then teachers need the support from their school administration to evaluate these skills properly.

There is the belief that a student who can obtain 80s and higher, has the proper skill set and work habits to achieve all excellent rating; consequently, that is not always the case. Sometimes students with 80s sill have areas where they need to improve and coincidentally there are some students who lack the same cognitive capabilities, but who work extremely hard, have a positive attitude, who are organized and take responsibility for their learning but fail to achieve the same grades. Learning skills should be evaluated based on the actual individual skills and not on their actual mark. They are independent of one another we should treat them as such.

The issue that was raised by the principal would be that some parents would be confused or upset if their child had 80s and yet received a few needs improvement. The same could be said about parents with children who achieve in the 50s or 60s and receive a few excellent in their learning skills. If parents notice a perceived discrepancy it would likely lead to some dialogue between parent and teacher. It could lead to a parent being confused because they would assume their child's grades and learning skills should match up with one another. Increasing dialogue between parents and teachers can only lead to positive discussions with the hopes of improving relationships between parents and teachers. If learning skills are to be included in report cards then they need to be conducted and evaluated effectively to get the most out of our students. We have these policies to evaluate students' success and improvement, but yet we are encouraged to not use these tools properly all with the hopes to make the numbers look better. The only number we should truly care about is the student's Ontario Education Number (OEN). Each student has a number attached to them from elementary school and it should be this number we care about, caring about each student as opposed to caring about numbers that make principals, boards, and the government look good. The priority should be on our students and their actual education and not on the government officials or school administrators. It is time to end the rhetoric and start the real learning.

DUE DATES

In the real world due dates are all around us; whether it is to pay a credit card or to apply for a job there are expectations placed on society to follow or risk paying a late penalty or missing out on a particular job. Due dates are vital and they surround our everyday lives which need to be taken seriously. Consequently, the education system is counterintuitive to this belief because due dates in Ontario's schools is only important for teachers to submit their marks on time, but meaningless to students. Even time management for students is an antiquated idea and largely because we allow this behaviour to continue. We as responsible adults are becoming very irresponsible when it comes to our youth by setting them up for failure. We constantly overlook all sorts of behaviours because as many will say, "pick your battles" or "don't sweat the small stuff" we need to focus on the little things so they do not become large issues. If we can prevent little things from happening and doing it early on, then it will make a difference in eliminating many of the bigger issues that consume our lives and the lives of Ontario's students.

Throughout schools when the bell rings that is usually when the students are walking into class. We try to implement school and class rules regarding tardiness but when there are no real consequences they simply continue to be late. Students need to understand that when the bell rings they should be at their seats and ready to begin class. Running into class as the bell is ringing is not considered on time because they are not prepared for class. I often ask students who of them have part time jobs to help rationalize to them my point of coming to class prepared and ready to start when the bell rings. I ask them, "if you are supposed to start work at 5:00pm that means you are expected to be dressed and ready at 5:00pm. Running into work at that time means technically you are late". Even though they see my point they refuse to buy into it because it goes against their belief system of what is expected of them at school. We need to change this ideological thinking that school is not like the real world. School should be treated like the real world—a progressive step on the ladder of our lives. Getting to work and school on time and following due dates should be an essential part of student training. There is a course in high schools called "Learning Strategies (GLS) but what they are learning in these courses is that time management and getting your work done on time is not important because it is so readily permitted in classrooms across Ontario.

Much of the issues that plague Ontario's students in terms of their work habits and output go back to the lack of consequences they face for their total apathy of their school work. When there are no consequences there is no need to strive for excellence. High school students are constantly faced with due dates for their assignments, or tests and yet even though every teacher will post due dates somewhere in the classroom and many are using technology to inform students of due dates, many students rarely ever complete their work on time.

There are numerous steps teachers take to attempt to get students to complete their assignments by the due dates. There are even drop dead dates where assignments not handed in by such dates would garner a zero. In theory, that is the goal to scare students into completing their assignments. It is not unheard of where an assignment is due in March with a drop dead date at the end of April and yet still many students refuse to submit their work by then. In the meantime, the teacher is expected to do more work because the students do not do their work. Because students do not do what they are expected to do, teachers are expected to do more work. What often happens is the teacher calls home to inform parents about the lack of work their son or daughter has submitted. The teacher has to explain to the parent why their son or daughter's marks are as low as they are. Sometimes contacting parents does improve the situation and these particular students do complete their work. Sadly, it does not work every time. In these situations, teachers need to take further actions to encourage students to complete their assignment by giving them lunch detention and having them stay in class with them to get some work done. By doing this the teacher gives up their lunch period to assist students to get their work done in order for them to be successful. Teachers often give up their lunch time or time before or after school so they can do all they can to help their students be successful. Nevertheless, this does not always work because the individual student must be present during lunch time detention for this process to be effective.

When these attempts fail to encourage students to complete their assignments teachers need to follow up with the students' success team by having students leave class and go to a quiet area to get their work done with the assistance of a student success teacher. In this case, the student success teacher has to figuratively hold the student's hand to complete his or her work. In many cases, these same students have a GLS or GLE course which means they are put in a class with a handful of other students where they go everyday to get work done from other classes. Essentially, these students get an additional credit for simply doing their homework for their other classes—just another way to give out credits. These courses are learning strategies courses; ironically, the strategies they are learning in courses such as these are that they can still be successful for doing nothing and continue to do nothing so others will do it for them. In these courses, students work at their own pace which is normally at a snail's pace, with a classroom teacher providing assistance. At the end of the semester, these students get a credit for simply doing what they should be doing in their regular classes. What this teaches students is procrastination and avoidance is perfectly acceptable.

Focus Period

The Near North District School Board has implemented a few strategies to help students in their workload. A way to combat this problem, many high schools within the board put into operation some time during the day specifically for students to get time to complete their homework. In some schools they call it MSIP (Multi Subject Instructional Period) where for one hour every day, students go to a classroom with the intended purpose of getting additional assistance and time to complete their work. It is intended for students to remain quiet in class to get work done. If by chance a student has no work to do they are to use this time to read quietly. Instead of having 4, 75 minute periods a day, schools that use MSIP have 5, 60 minute periods where one hour is dedicated to acquire extra help and to complete their school work. In theory this direction for providing students the adequate time and assistance to get their work done is very admirable because it has the student's best interest in mind, but again like everything else it needs to work properly to be an effective tool for student success. The glaring issues with MSIP and the way it is implemented is that students from all grades are placed in a class with a teacher that may not be their own. What often happens is a teacher will get students who are having difficulties with a particular subject say Math and the MSIP teacher is not Math qualified or even have adequate knowledge to assist students in the subject. In this case, students are then given permission to leave the MSIP class and find their subject teacher to get the assistance they require to complete their homework. What often occurs is the student will be granted permission to leave the MSIP class and wander the halls because they need to find their teacher. The issue then becomes one of congestion in the halls as many students are not actually looking for their teacher but more for friends to hang out with. They get away with it when stopped by a teacher by simply informing that teacher they are on their way to get assistance. It then becomes extremely loud in the halls with students wandering around wasting time. With the advent of the cell phone and texting, students just text each other to get out of their classes and meet up and at times problems occur because too many students are in the halls as opposed to being in their class getting their work done. For MSIP to be effective there needs to be a better policy in how it is run and how the school will administer the proper use of MSIP. It cannot continue the way it is going as far too much time is being wasted wandering the halls and distracting others who are working.

The other issue with MSIP is that for the most part what is going on in the class is not effective use of class time as some students simply use the time to play games on their phones. Many teachers will not say much if students are wasting their time as long as they are quiet. As long as students are relatively quiet they can continue to play their games or go on Facebook or whatever as long as they are not being disruptive. As was mentioned earlier, the MSIP teacher is often not their regular teacher so they are not necessarily invested in the students' work or even have an idea what work the students may still have owing for other teachers. Also, some teachers use the quiet time to get their own work done. It could act as time to do some marking or preparing for up-coming lessons. There is time specifically for students to complete work or get additional help with their school work but what ends up happening is students have more time to waste and disrupt all because there is no consequence for this behaviour. The more time they get to complete work, the more time they waste. Students are normally given some class time with their teacher to get work done, they get MSIP time to get work done and yet the amount of late assignments is astounding. There should never be any late assignments because of all this time given to them. What needs to take place is a more stringent set of rules for students who hand in late work. This behaviour should not be allowed to continue and not be so readily acceptable.

Not all schools in the Near North District School Board have the MSIP period in their schools. Parry Sound High School for instance has a similar program that they do but they call it 'focus' period. Originally, Parry Sound High School functioned on a 4 day week so each class would get their turn at having a focus period. The second period of the day would have the focus period attached to it. The students would have a brief 5 minute break and then return to the class for the one hour focus period. The entire focus was on students getting any one-on-one help with their classroom teacher or spending the time working on completing their school work. The focus period worked relatively well because the students would be in the class with their teacher so any help needed would be available. The class was not a hodgepodge of different students from different grades. It was geared towards student success. The students would spend the first hour of the class for instruction period and then a break then a focus period to get any work done. The goal was to get that particular class' work done first and if it was they could work on other class' assignments if they had time. The one issue with this policy was often students became tired because they would spend two hours in the same classroom. So for the first part of focus period some students would get some work done and then half way through they would begin to get restless and start chatting with their friends. This then prevents the teacher from focusing on providing small group instruction for students who require it. Often the teacher had to focus on maintaining classroom management.

Two years ago, Parry Sound High School decided to go to a two day week for the purpose of changing the focus period with the hope of making it more effective for all students and teachers. There would be two periods in the morning and two in the afternoon which would alternate between the two days. Instead of having a one hour focus period, the school principal decided to have two 30 minute focus period. One would be in the morning and one would be in the afternoon. The policy would remain that the focus period would be strictly for the students to receive additional help from the teacher and to get their work done.

In making the changes from a four day week at Parry Sound High School to a two day week would make it easier for the students to remember what day it was. It also gave more attention towards focus periods because they were down to 30 minutes for each period which means less time for students to become tired and lose focus on their work and coincidentally less time for classroom disruption. Also, during focus period, a student could be sent to a computer lab which was called

"The Hub" where students could use computers if needed while under the supervision of the Hub teacher. The classroom teacher would have to sign an admit slip for the student to go and then the Hub teacher would have to sign it when the student left so both teachers were aware when each student were expected to attend the Hub. They would also have to sign into the computer to maintain a record of how many students use the Hub every day. Which also served as a backup in case the student did not get the permission slipped signed or they lost it. The classroom teacher could simply access the computer records to see when the students arrived and left. The policy was fairly well run and the intended purpose was solely for student success. Sadly, even though the policy was sound it did not produce the numbers expected as far too many students were still not completing their assignments in a timely fashion because many were spending their time on Facebook. It is believed that Facebook should be one of the websites that is blocked in schools. By blocking access, it would help alleviate some of the time wasted on the website. Schools are doing everything in their power to ensure students success and trying to implement policies to give every student the best possible chance to succeed.

When students fail to do what is expected of them it falls onto the teacher to do more work; like filling out forms on the number of students who are failing or on the verge of failing because of their lack of work submitted. Teachers have to exhaust all sorts of avenues to get students to complete their work. This is often a month after the due date has passed and still the teacher is working on getting students to hand in their assignments. It is a huge problem for every high school in Ontario. Instead of enforcing some rules and sticking with them, we allow students to continue this path of apathy towards their education.

In 2010, the school where I was teaching decided to implement some late penalties to students who failed to submit their work. It was assumed that if there were penalties and consequences it would help eliminate the problem of students not completing their work. In theory, implementing these rules could help in minimizing the high amount of students who refuse to submit their work because in the past students earned the same mark whether they handed it in on the due date or two months late. This ideology teaches that due dates are not important and let us not forget that it is not necessarily fair to the students who do submit their work on time. In an attempt to avoid this situation, the school decided that late penalty marks should be implemented. It was decided that students in grade 9 and 10 could be penalized a maximum of 15% and students in grade 11 and 12 could face 30% in late penalty marks. This policy would better prepare students who eventually would be going to college or university because at the post-secondary level they do implement penalties on late assignments. This is a sound decision to attempt to change students' mindset of homework completion and to hope bring back an importance to proper work habits. It would not instantly change the students' mentality because they did have those bad habits of the past. However, for the policy of late penalties to truly work it would have to be enforced and maintained over a long period of time. Our students have been trained that due dates and late penalties do not matter so it will take time to change their thinking. Regardless how long and tedious the process takes educators have to stand pat and maintain the late penalty policy for it to work.

The issue that is detrimental to the idea of imposing late penalty marks to students, who grossly misuse their time management, is the policy that students cannot fail a grade because of late penalty marks. The idea of showing them there are consequences to not following due dates will greatly help them throughout their life. Due dates are imposed and need to be followed. It is good practice to teach students that there are expectations and consequences they will face if they do not comply with. Imposing due dates on students but not enforcing the consequences is absolutely pointless and a waste of time and effort because students learn that it does not matter what their teachers say because they know in the end that it is simply empty threats. With that said, even if a student in grade 9 or 10 ends the course with a 42% with the 15% late penalties their marks are just getting bumped up to 50% anyways. We have these late penalties to teach students some responsibilities; nonetheless, they understand that regardless what is said about consequences they know how things work within the education system. By continuously telling students they have expectations and if they do not reach them they will suffer the consequences but yet not follow through gives the students the appearance that teachers have no credibility within the education system and have no authority in our children's lives. We need to follow through with the rules we implement to begin to regain some form of credibility with our youth.

We have to obey the rules of the road set for us and if a driver goes through a red light there are consequences that will be enforced and as a result all drivers know to follow the rules and come to a stop or face a monetary fine. If the law was in place but the police did not enforce the law then how many drivers do you think would go through red lights? Even though there would be a risk of an accident some drivers would still go through red lights because of the lack of law enforcement preventing drivers from obeying the law. That is essentially what the education system does we implement rules but do not enforce them. Our Ontario students are going through the red lights of their education. The accident they face is the atrophy of their lifelong learning.

In senior grades of grade 11 and 12, students can face late penalties of up to 30% as a way to illustrate to them the importance of taking responsibility for their actions of completing their school assignments. Some of the students have the intention of heading off to college or university and with the lack of importance of due dates in high school it will be disastrous for them in post-secondary. This is why it is vital to express to them why it is important to take responsibility. We need to get them accustomed to using their time more wisely when they are off to post-secondary because they will face late penalties and real late penalties that will be enforced. By not preparing them in high school for what is to come in college and university is doing our Ontario students are great disservice because we cannot expect them to instantly change their thinking over a course of one summer. These students have been taught and trained that not following the rules of work habits is perfectly acceptable in elementary and high school then we send them off into the world blindfolded. Whether students are heading off to college, university or the workforce it should be instilled in them that proper work habits are essential for future success. Due dates and deadlines need to be taken seriously. In university, there are late penalties imposed for each day their work is not submitted. If students do not do the work, they get a zero. Inevitably it will eventually lead to the cry of unfairness taking place because they were totally unprepared for life after high school.

For students in high school who lack the necessary marks to pass a course on their own they are offered one final chance to complete assignments. A team of teachers are compiled to make telephone calls home to inform parents that during exam time their child can come in to get any outstanding work completed in order to get their credit. Regardless of due dates or deadlines, teachers have no choice but to accept the work for final evaluation. What often happens is students come in and spend very little time and effort on their assignment simply to hand something in and with that they are expected to get whatever mark is needed for the student to pass and not get a mark that is deserving of the actual output of their work. Yet again, teaching our students bad habits in their work ethic. The disconcerting aspect is this last desperate gambit to hand something in is usually far below expectations and should not be given a good grade, it should be graded based on value, and not on what is needed to 'earn' a passing grade. Although, does it really matter since a 41% gets bumped up to 50% anyways. That is 41% now who is to say that in the next two years that number drops to 38% or lower. Our students 'earn' a passing grade for work well below expectations so they believe that kind of work is completely acceptable to 'earn' a passing grade in high schools throughout Ontario. It is unfathomable that the leaders of this province truly believe that the current direction of the education system is on the proper path of lifelong learning for Ontario's students.

PATHWAYS FOR ONTARIO

There are such complex issues going on in Ontario and throughout the world for that matter. The economy in Ontario is facing cuts; the provincial government is dealing with cuts to government expenditures. A few European nations are on the brink of total collapse and yet our leaders have no clear direction in how to properly prepare our students for complex economic issues that they will inevitably face in the future. We need to prepare them for whatever pathway they choose for themselves or have it chosen for them. What I mean by this is what they may want may not be what they get because of lack of skills, or bad habits that were not dealt with while in high school. With so much economic uncertainty with what is going to happen in ten years let alone next year students need to grasp some understanding of how difficult things can become without a clear path in mind. We live in an ever changing global world and things change quickly and we need to be flexible, willing and able to accept change and almost be able to predict it before it happens. It is integral to help alleviate the stress when it undoubtedly arises.

As a result of the clear uncertainty that consumes our lives it is not enough to simply obtain an education. That piece of paper is worthless if there is no knowledge behind the paper. It will be meaningless if our students who acquire it cannot compete in the real world. The disheartening matter is these pieces of paper are being given away without any real work being done to earn it. Our education system has been continuously devaluing an Ontario Secondary School Diploma with no regard for the consequences.

There lacks a discernible direction within the education system in Ontario where we are unsure what direction we really should focus on for our students. Twenty years ago, the push was for students to concentrate on a university education because getting a degree was what would give our students the utmost chance at a lifetime of professional success. If someone wanted to be successful he or she needed to go to university—or that is what many thought. That is not to say that direction in today's world would be wrong—not at all because a university degree is still vital for the future success of Ontario and its students.

This is where our education system has been going around in circles chasing its own metaphorical tail and not making a dent in the progress that is needed for our future. If we are going to focus on the university path for our students then we need to prepare them to be successful. We need to get back to teaching systematic purposes in properly teaching them work ethic and taking pride in what they produce. This process will not be repaired overnight. It will take a lot of time and effort from Ontario's provincial government and Ontario's educators. Our students will only buy into a restructured education system if their role models buy into—which means all stakeholders, parents, teachers and administrators need to play a part in improving the education system. We have to get the Minister of Education on board and not worry what is going on in other provinces or what is taking place in the United States. It is obvious there are issues with the education system throughout North America. I am confident that any changes we do will not make things worse than they are right now. We need to take the initiative like we expect from our own students and make the necessary changes for the amelioration of Ontario's students. If our changes become isolated to this province then we could take pride in knowing we made changes to our education with the hopes of making a positive improvement for our children. By making the changes we could also be viewed as innovators and give our youth an advantage over other students across the country. We want to bestow the best opportunity to our students to become leaders in this global world.

If our educational system is going to continue pushing students towards a university education then we need to begin early on in their academic lives to expect proper work ethic from our students. This is something that is expected of university students so why not teach them that early on. Why should we set them up for failure? We can no longer allow mediocrity from them. In order to get them accustomed to working hard and taking pride in their work we need to enforce the belief that working properly is important and expected of them. If they do not do their work properly and as expected they should be expected to redo it until it is done properly. We should never settle for work that is below our expectations and below what our students can produce. We need to forgo the idea of thinking we are harming our students' self-esteem by placing higher expectations on our students instead of just allowing them to skate by. That ideological thinking is not working nor will it ever work so why are we continuing to follow that type of belief? This type of behaviour has been going on for the last decade or so and it is getting worse. The education system needs to take some responsibility and expect more from our students. If we raise the bar they will reach for it. The problem is we have set the bar so low that our students have no incentive to reaching for anything more than mediocrity. We need to enforce due dates and get students back on their educational track. This "hug a thug" mentality with our students needs to come to an end. What the education system and society for that matter needs to bring back is some "tough love" and show our students we care enough to want the best for them.

I strongly believe we are doing a great injustice to the students who do not plan on attending university after high school. There are so many students in this province that could become very successful in their career aspirations, but not in terms of a university degree. Ontario has an abundance of students who would excel in the skilled trades; conversely, many schools have either cut the program altogether or minimized its importance within their school. The Ministry of Education should refocus on these particular students because for many of them we are leaving them behind—something that is counter to the ideological rhetoric of no child left behind.

We have a great number of students who do not do well in specific literature courses where students are expected to read Shakespearean plays or classical books such as <u>To Kill A Mockingbird</u> so they take applied or college level English classes. Nevertheless even in college level English courses the students do in fact study plays and novels something that does little in way to interest these students. This is not to say that English is not important for students who want to enter trades schools throughout this province just that curriculum needs to be refocused for specific pathways. The Ministry of Education needs to modify curriculum for specific pathways to gear education specifically for specific students. At the moment, the pathway is university, college or the workforce, which is fine but curriculum should be more centered towards their needs. Maybe if curriculum was focused on precise pathways it is possible that more students would be more engaged in their own education. At the moment, we have schools filled with disengaged students.

The students who desire to attend university after high school should be expected to understand how to properly write essays as this will be something they will likely be spending much of their time doing while in university, depending on what courses they take. There are courses at the university level that will expect students to think critically and conceptualize and contextualize their learning and that is something that Ontario high school students lack when they enter their first year of university. Our students need to acquire the ability to have comprehensible reading skills with the aptitude to think critically. The curriculum as it is now could remain the same as it is geared towards the pathway to university—we just need some changes to what we teach our students and what we expect from our students.

For students who have no intention of attending university the curriculum should be focused on their pathway. Studying Shakespeare may not benefit these particular students because learning about Hamlet may not necessarily prove beneficial for students who aspire to become mechanics or plumbers. The English these students should acquire is that which will benefit them in the skilled trades. They should learn to write properly with emphasis on spelling and how to communicate in a clear and concise manner for their specific purpose. They do not need to know how to write essays they need to know how to write purchase orders and how to communicate estimates in written form. There should be an emphasis on math classes with a focus on taxes and of course their Ontario Secondary School Diploma should be geared towards more trades courses than literature courses. The mandatory 30 credits should continue to be the standard to graduate but the direction of where the credits come from should be more specific for certain areas within their curriculum needs.

Sadly, what often happens to students that have a passion for shop class or mechanics class do not have the same desire for classes such as English or history classes. They are obligated to take these courses therefore they become very distraught with their own academic achievements. The courses that they are forced to take are not geared towards their own academic and post-secondary goals. It is understood that courses like history and geography should remain in the curriculum for all students just that maybe courses like English should be more geared towards students whose ambition it is to enter the skilled trades. Many of these students lose interest in school or are seen as low achievers within the realm of academia simply because they may not have the cognitive ability or desire to excel in classes where it is not hands-on. The idea that these particular students lack the necessary intelligence could not be further from the truth because many skilled tradespeople are highly intelligent. The perception that these students lack the same cognitive development as their peers at the university level is what has been grossly misunderstood over the last few decades. This type of thinking needs to be changed because of the importance that skilled tradespeople play within our society now and in the future.

The skill trades are facing a devastating shortage of skilled tradespeople and for the next twenty years it will continue to get worse if we do not place a larger focus on directing our students to that pathway. This is where we are doing our students and our future a great disservice because we have not encouraged more tactile learning of the skilled trades. There is nothing in elementary school to help students find that passion unless they have a family member who inspires that passion within them. Years ago, a few elementary schools had some shop classes where students could build a shelf, a coat rack or any other little thing that could get the students excited about building something with their hands. It may not have been a regular class but at least elementary students were experiencing building at an early age. The desire has to come early on because if it is not there by high school chances are it will never be there. I understand the world we live in is far different from what it was years ago. Today, there are too many liabilities to have such programs because of the legal ramifications if an accident were to happen. We as a society are too afraid to do anything because of what might happen. Yes, accidents are bad and when they do it is extremely sad but we cannot stop living just because we fear getting sued. Maybe our legal system needs to be adjusted as well. These trivial law suits must be stopped before they begin. When Macdonald's was sued because their coffee was too hot was the beginning of the end to our common sense in the legal world. Many things must change before we can get back to bringing shop classes back in the elementary curriculum because as it stands the liability cost will be far too much for school boards to take on. So at the moment students lack the understanding and desire for shop class as many do not even know how to hold a hammer.

When students enter grade 9 many lack the passion, desire and knowledge to take shop classes and some only take a course because they believe it is a "bird" course. The students who do have the skill and passion likely acquired it from a family member prior to starting high school. These students tend to work hard and the students who feel it is a "bird" course spend the majority of their time goofing off. Shop classes should be the last place where goofing off takes place because of the obvious dangers. The skilled trades' classes in high schools should be valued much more than they currently are. Many of the students who show a lack of interest in school excel in the skilled trades classes which is why the education system should place a greater importance for the benefit of our students and for the future success of Ontario. We talk about differented instruction all the time because not all kids learn the same which is so true, so why is our education system not making the necessary adjustments for differented learning, so all students even those who learn differently can have the same chance at becoming successful? We have to learn to teach students differently, essentially we are teaching the same to everyone only differently. Students who may lack interest in the current curriculum are not taught what interests them. They simply are pushed along so our education system can get the numbers they strive for. It does not really matter what kind of education our students are getting as long as they get that precious piece of paper at the end. Some students despise English classes and do not do well in them but take that same student and put him or her in a shop class and they will build you a kitchen cabinet or a coffee table perfectly well and do so in very little time. These particular students strive for this type of classroom and should be encouraged to further their passion by providing these students with options so they will want to attain skilled trades at the college level. We need to get them interested in their education so we do not lose them along the way. Many of these students end up obtaining their Ontario Secondary School Diploma but do so in obscurity as they leave high school with a piece of paper but no transferable skills or desire to become productive members of society.

If a student shows an interest and skill in writing we provide him or her additional resources to further that passion by taking more literature courses. When a student shows a passion in the skilled trades there is not the same opportunities for her or him. We need to re-evaluate the education system and open the doors to different pathways to make it more conducive for all of our students to be successful. They need to feel successful, not just giving them their high school diploma and telling them they have been successful. Success is not success if students leave high school with a piece of paper but are no better off then when they entered. They need to acquire knowledge that will help them on their own personal journey to a successful life whether that is through university, college or the workforce.

What I suggest is a complete overhaul of what is deemed necessary to earn an Ontario Secondary School Diploma. For students who would chose this path, then there should be some type of differiented Instruction as in what they learn as well as how they learn it. As opposed to having a student's require four English credits maybe it should be cut down to two or three and the English curriculum should be geared towards teaching appropriate English content for students in the skilled trades program. I know curriculum is pretty open as teachers have options to teach what they like as long as they teach curriculum. Instead of teaching Shakespearean plays to college level English courses they should teach something more appropriate for these students. Even though many of the plays that are being taught are in graphic novel form it may not be content geared to these particular students. Instead of teaching them about Shakespeare or how to write a short story or poetry, the English instruction these students should be getting should be geared to what they need and use in college and in the workforce. I do not know too many carpenters or plumbers who spend much of their time discussing any Shakespearean discourse while on the job.

If curriculum was centered more towards individual pathways maybe it would improve how much our students are learning and maybe, just maybe our students would begin to fully become lifelong learners. We need to not spend the majority of our focus on what is trending—this is not Twitter, this is our students' future we need to give them the best possible opportunity to be successful. Technology is taking over that does not mean we should move away from the skilled trades in favour of using technology to entertain our students. We are not in the entertainment business; we are in the educating business.

Instead of focusing on the trend of technological devices such as iPads and smartphones and every other device to entertain Ontario's students we need to converge on what is needed in this province which is skilled tradespeople. As ubiquitous as technology is society still requires tradespeople and at the moment there is a dramatic shortfall which is only getting worse. It has been reported that there will be a "shortfall of one million skilled tradespeople in Canada by the year 2020" (MacLean's). If this is true and by all accounts it appears to be, we need to rectify this situation right now instead of waiting until the damage is done. The people who will be close to retirement will be encouraged not to retire because of the shortfall. What is sure to happen is unskilled labour will be forced to do skilled trades' work which could lead to more accidents or deaths because of the inexperience in such skilled positions! The other option that is likely to occur is these skilled trades jobs will be gobbled up by Asians and Middle Eastern people because they are not afraid to work as it has been engrained in them from an early age. Really, I do not see why companies would not hire Asians and Middle Eastern people because for the most part one of them amounts to three of us because they do not shy away from long hours or hard work. We have taught our children that avoiding work is perfectly acceptable so when it comes down to the hiring process our children will be overlooked time and time again in favour of their Asian and Middle Eastern counterparts.

This is not to suggest that all Ontario students are lazy, just that a large portion of our youth have not had the proper work ethic engrained in them. Our education system has failed in teaching our students that hard work pays off, and for many that same teaching has not been there for them at home either. Parents and teachers need to show our youth that working hard will benefit them throughout their entire lives. If this ends up to be the case where Asians and Middle Eastern people dominate our skilled trades then it will lead to a sense of unfairness and jealousy by Ontario's students which could very well lead to racial and ethnic animosity and strife towards certain ethnical groups. This animosity will not stem from anything that Asians and Middle Eastern people have done aside from being taught, at an early age, to work hard.

In the August 25, 2011 issue of MacLean's Magazine, Cynthia Reynolds wrote that in 2009, "a poll showed one-third of teens spend zero time per week doing anything hands-on. Instead, by one account, entertainment media eats up 53 hours a week for kids aged eight to 18." That is 53 hours per week, more than most people work per week. Our students our spending this time on their cell phones texting, Facebook, Twitter or other social media networks and playing video games. Even if they cut 10 hours of that number they would have all their school work and maybe even some quality time with family members doing fun family things. This number spent on entertainment media begs the question—where are parents during this time? Is it just easier having their children occupied with social media then it is to spend time with one another or even with their friends? This number is staggering and brings to light why so many of our youth are overweight, unhealthy and always tired.

The old days of working on the car with dad are long gone which is truly sad that our society has come to this. Children are more focused on their phones, computer and video games then they are with being outside. Our youth are no longer getting valuable time with dad learning how to build things with their hands. What is happening is our children are only trying these things once they reach high school and some of those are only taking these courses for the wrong reasons. Many of our students are not getting the required knowledge to be successful in the skilled trades or are starting later on in their lives. They are not learning the basics at an early age like many had years ago. This just leads to a decline in trades courses at the high school level which then becomes a revolving cycle of less and less importance placed on skilled trades in Ontario high schools. We need to find a way to get students interested at an earlier age whether it is at home or in elementary school.

The skills our students have is in technology, the majority of them know how to navigate through a Smartphone, and computer and programs associated with technological devices. Our students lack the ability and skill to work with their hands as well as lack the ability or desire to be meticulous in their work ethic. Many simply do not care. "They don't know how to handle a tool properly, Barry Smith says quietly, they're bright kids, but they hold a hammer at the top instead of the bottom, so it takes four swings instead of one to get a nail in. They don't know how to read the short lines on a tape measure and they've never used power tools, which makes you really cautious. He says they can't seem to detect the patterns of the work—you rip up part of the roof, that gets thrown down, that goes into the garbage—so they just stand around. It can get really frustrating" (Reynolds, MacLean's). The level of frustration felt by tradespeople like Barry Smith of Roofsmith Canada a roofing company in the Toronto area is becoming a constant issue throughout because our youth do not value the idea of hard work or even trying to understand what is needed to be successful in whatever they do. It is hard to blame them entirely because throughout their lives they have not been taught to get their work done or to take pride in the work they do. They have been skating by on mediocrity all their life and do not understand what it takes in the workforce. What often happens is they get fired because of their poor work ethic and then do not know how to cope with disappointment. Their home life and school life has set them up for disappointment.

"One auto shop teacher says he teaches his Grade 12 students what, 10 years ago, he taught Grade Nines. We would take apart a transmission, now I teach what it is. If he introduces a nut treaded counter clockwise, they have trouble conceptualizing the need to turn the screwdriver the opposite way. That's because, he says, they're texting non-stop; they don't care about anything else. It's like they're possessed" (Reynolds, MacLean's). Their hands are now used to holding their Smartphones instead of a hammer and their fingers spend their time texting instead of writing. Fine motor skills are being lost because of the lack of importance of writing with pens and pencils in favour of technological devices.

Occupational therapist Stacy Kramer, clinical director at Toronto's Hand Skills for Children, offers one explanation for what's happening. It begins with babies who don't get put on the ground as much, which means less crawling, less hand development. Then comes the litany of push-button toy gadgets, which don't exercise the whole hand. That leads to difficulty developing skills that require a more intricate coordination between the hand and brain, like holding a pencil or using scissors, which kindergarten teachers complain more students can't do. "We see 13-year-olds who can't do up buttons or tie laces," she says. "Parents just avoid it by buying Velcro and T-shirts." Items that—not incidentally—chimpanzees could put on.

Predictably, this is affecting other industries that depend on a mechanically inclined workforce. After NASA's Jet Propulsion Lab noticed its new engineers couldn't do practical problem solving the way its retirees could, it stopped hiring those who didn't have mechanical hobbies in their youth. When MIT realized its engineering students could no longer estimate solutions to problems on their own, that they needed their computers, it began adding remedial building classes to better prepare these soon-to-be professionals for real-world jobs, like designing airplanes and bridges. Architecture schools are also adding back-to-basics courses. As for the trades? Veterans like Barry Smith have little choice but to attempt to nurse a hands-on ability among new recruits one hammer faux pas at a time, teaching the next generation of tradespeople just how to hit a nail on the head (Reynolds, MacLean's).

This information should not be a surprise to the Ministry of Education and our current provincial government that our students are failing in the basics of hands-on work and they are failing in their ability to write properly. In what direction are these students excelling in besides social media? Our education system and society as a whole is grossly misleading our youth down a path of obscurity and metaphorical extinction. They are losing their cognitive ability to function independently; they lack critical thinking skills and the ability to take any initiative. If we need to revamp the entire educational process to make the necessary changes then that is what is needed because our future depends on it. It is clear that the skilled trades are in dire need of new recruits whether those recruits come from Ontario or elsewhere they will need to be replaced. Asians and Middle Eastern people have strong work ethic and the ability to adapt to current needs and societal demands of a workforce. Our government, as well as all citizens of this fine province needs to stop enabling our children's apathy. The only thing they will show any interests in is their cell phones, and social media and that is because we continue to allow them to act in such a way. The more we permit this to happen the worse it is going to get. Let them roll their eyes at us; let them give us attitude because we no longer allow them to hold us hostage because that is essentially what they are doing—holding us hostage. We fear our youth because of the power we have given them. We allow them to threaten us with these nonsensical threats of calling the Children's Aid Society simply because they do not get what they want. It is time we take the power back.

DROP-OUT RATES

Back a couple of decades ago, drop-out rates for high school students were slightly higher than they are now. To look at the surface it illustrates a positive trend when only looking at the statistics. Conversely, when we look deeper that is where the issues persist. Just because drop-out rates look better it does not mean it is better. We need to remove the smoke screen that shrouds our understanding of what is truly going within our current education system in Ontario. From the years between 1990 and 1993, the national drop-out rate for high school students was 15.7%. From 2002 to 2005, the rate dropped down to 10.1%. The drop-out rates in Ontario during the same period between 1990 and 1993 was 14.7%, and 9.1% between 2002 and 2005, and 7.8% between 2007 and 2010. The following information was taken directly from the Stats Can website.

Table 1: Thousands of drop-outs[1] and drop-out rate, Canada, 1990-1991 to 2004-2005 school year averages

	Thousands	Drop-out rate (%)
1990-1991	337.8	16.7
1991-1992	320.3	15.9
1992-1993	289.8	14.5
1993-1994	279.2	14.1
1994-1995	265.0	13.5
1995-1996	245.9	12.6
1996-1997	237.7	12.1
1997-1998	242.4	12.3
1998-1999	223.3	11.3
1999-2000	230.0	11.5

2000-2001	225.6	11.1
2001-2002	223.9	10.8
2002-2003	228.4	10.8
2003-2004	207.7	9.7
2004-2005	212.3	9.8

[1] Defined as 20-24-year-olds without a high school diploma and not in school.

Source: Statistics Canada, Labour Force Survey.

Table 2: Thousands of drop-outs[1] and drop-out rate, Canada and provinces, 1990-1991 to 1992-1993 and 2002-2003 to 2004-2005 school year averages[2]

	1990-1991 to 1992-1993		2002-2003 to 2004-2005	
	Thousands	Drop-out rate (%)	Thousands	Drop-out rate (%)
Canada	316.0	15.7	216.2	10.1
Newfoundland and Labrador	10.0	20.0	2.8	8.0
Prince Edward Island	1.8	19.1	0.9	9.7
Nova Scotia	12.0	17.9	5.7	9.3
New Brunswick	8.6	15.4	4.5	9.2
Quebec	84.3	17.4	60.1	11.9
Ontario	114.2	14.7	74.8	9.1
Manitoba	12.5	16.1	9.9	13.0
Saskatchewan	10.4	16.3	7.3	10.7
Alberta	30.8	15.8	28.8	12.0
British Columbia	31.5	13.3	21.2	7.5

Table 1

Number of dropouts1 and dropout rate, provinces, 1990/1993 and 2007/2010

	1990/1993		2007/2010	
	thousands	**percent**	**thousands**	**percent**
Newfoundland and Labrador	10.0	19.9	2.2	7.4
Prince Edward Island	1.8	18.9	0.9	8.9
Nova Scotia	11.9	17.8	5.2	8.6
New Brunswick	8.6	15.4	3.8	8.1
Quebec	84.2	17.4	55.5	11.7
Ontario	114.3	14.8	68.6	7.8
Manitoba	12.4	16.0	9.1	11.4
Saskatchewan	10.4	16.2	6.7	9.4
Alberta	30.7	15.7	28.3	10.4
British Columbia	31.5	13.3	19.1	6.2

1 defined as 20-to 24-year-olds without a high school diploma and not in school

Note: due to small sample sizes in many provinces, all provincial data are based on a

3-year average (1990/1993 and 2007/2010).

Source: Statistics Canada, Labour Force Survey.

As you can see from the previous tables the numbers are looking better and better with the recent decline in the drop-out rates with high school students. However that is a myopic view that our governing bodies who control our education system would like us to believe. The real numbers that need to be looked into is the number of students who are dropping out of college and university because they have not been prepared for life after high school. The high school drop-out numbers may appear positive but that is simply because of the ease in acquiring a high school diploma leaves students no real need to drop-out. As long as they show up on occasion they will be successful in obtaining their Ontario Secondary School Diploma. With the ease it is to obtain an Ontario Secondary School Diploma in today's world 81% success rate is not actually all that impressive.

Another number that should be carefully investigated is the number of post-secondary students who commit suicide because of the stress of post-secondary or more from the expectations that are placed upon them because they will ill-prepared in high school. For many students, this is the first time they have any expectations placed on them and many simply cannot handle it, nor can they handle or know how to deal with difficult situations as they were never taught. This stress is something that they have never experienced because they were never expected to do much work in elementary or high school. We give our students that piece of paper that states they earned their Ontario Secondary School Diploma, but were never prepared for what was to come. This in no way means we have to make college and university easier or placate the learning expectations, it means we need to start placing stricter expectations on our students to fully prepare them and give them the skill and understanding of how to handle difficult situations. We need to teach our students how to be able to deal with stress in their lives and by placing some expectations on them earlier will help alleviate that stress later on. What our students have been taught for much of their lives is to avoid anything that may cause our students some stress; if we do not teach them properly the rate of suicides from our youth will climb dramatically. This is something I for one do not want to see.

Ontario high school students are entering colleges and universities without being properly prepared because many lack the ability to think critically and independently. Alan Slavin of university affairs.ca asked, "Has Ontario's educational system taught a decade of students not to think? A dramatic indication that there could be a serious problem was the performance of my introductory physics class. It was identical to one given in 1996, but the class average over this ten year period has plummeted from 66 to 50 percent" (Slavin). Considering it is the same test the numbers should remain fairly constant with some fluctuations up or down from year-to-year but overall it should remain within similar parameters as long as the education they receive in high school remains the same. It is fairly safe to say the level of education our students are receiving compared to students from twenty years ago has not changed all that much. What has changed is the level of work ethic and expectations. This is where the real problem lies.

In today's schools across the province our students are obtaining far higher grades then they deserve. As far as expectations go, it is we the educators who have lowered our expectation. Instead of insisting on students reach higher expectations we have come down and what would have earned a 65% two decades ago is now getting 10-15% higher in today's classrooms. Ontario's high school students are slowly walking out of high school with marks in the 80s and yet are doing very little work to earn it. Our students enter university with these lofty expectations and the same work ethic as they did in high school, but with devastative consequences. They get a very rude awakening when they receive their first assignment back to them with much lower marks then they have learned to expect from their years in high school. They do not know how to react and become angered by their "low" marks because either "it is not fair," "my professor hates me," or some other reason that they refuse to take responsibility for. In some cases, they are probably right because our education system has taught them this behaviour and after a few months at university they are expected to unlearn years of bad habits to be successful in college or university. This is where students decide whether they will find it in them to change their ways and take responsibility in their learning or just continue on their path of complacency and see what happens good or bad or simply dropout of college or university.

The first year of university can be an extremely great time because for a large portion it is the first time they are away from home. They are living on their own with no parents to nag them, but maybe they need to be nagged more otherwise they would not be in this situation. Consequently, there is no parent there to care for them as they are used to. They have to grow up fast and for many eighteen year olds it is too much to handle and many cannot cope with the struggles of first year university. They do enjoy the fun of the social setting that university life entails. The first few months of first year university life is analogous to a wolf being let loose in a chicken coup—very little good will come from it—but it will be fun.

The misconception which often dominates that discourse of why so many students drop out of university is because they are lazy. In some cases, this is extremely accurate, but it is not the case for all students. Yes, laziness and a lack of self-regulation do play a huge role in some student's inability to complete his or her first year of university. Nevertheless, it should not be the sole ideological reason why some students drop out before they complete their first year of university. What needs to be taken into account is their lack of preparedness which is the greater cause for the elevated dropout rate. "Todd Stinebrickner, a Western University economics professor explains on average, students enter university overly optimistic about their likely performance, predicting they will obtain far higher grades than what they actually obtain in the first semester. As a result many students learn over the course of their studies that university is not a good match for them academically, and they choose to drop out" (Western). This happens a lot as students believe going into university they will obtain the same marks as they did during high school all the while socializing even more than they ever did in previous years. Our students are being set up to fail by the very same people who should be engaging them to think for themselves. "They're not prepared for the heavier workload and independent study time. Things have to be a little bit different at earlier stages [of education], whether it is more effort in high school or a change in the quality of schools at earlier stages" (Globe and Mail). Whatever the answer is, it needs to be realized sooner rather than later otherwise our students will continue to show poorly while in university. We send our students out into the university and college life without properly preparing them for what they will expect. After the first month, many students get an eye opener and quickly realize that university life is far more difficult than they were accustomed in high school. We send our students out into the world smelling of blood which does not take long before the sharks of real life set in ready to strike.

The purpose of high school is to teach our students curriculum and to prepare them for either college, university or the workforce. By continually allowing our students to get away with apathy and complacency we are in all intent and purposes leaving them behind because life in high school will never be juxtaposed with life in college or university. They are leaving the nest without the ability to fly. "We're dealing with students who are overachievers in high school. They often have never had anything worse than an A, said Diane Fisher" (CTV. ca Sept 26). When students get 60s when they expect 80s it becomes difficult to adapt and make the necessary personal changes to ensure their success. They often do not know where to start to get the marks they were accustomed to receive in high school. The concern that many people have is the inability for our students to cope with stress, they have no coping mechanism when difficulties arise. "The university dropout rate was about 16 percent; in college or CEGEP, it was higher, at 25 percent" (Globecampus.ca). If our students were properly prepared in high school they would be able to deal with difficult situations when they are confronted with them as opposed to the standard reaction of depression and sorrow. They cannot deal with difficulties and if it means to dropout or quit their job then so be it. The majority of students coming out of high school will avoid any difficult or stressful situations at all cost because throughout their lives programs or other people did things to ease their life. Our society has trained our youth to avoid stressful situations and when confronted with them they react inappropriately which usually leads to the blame game or complaining about it not being fair. We have turned our youth into a group of people who feel a sense of entitlement. They need to strengthen their resolve to overcome any difficult situation they face. Nevertheless, this problem is only getting worse from the reported suicide rate from our youth.

In order to be proactive, many universities have implemented a fall reading week where classes shut down for a week to alleviate stress especially for first year students. Over the last couple of years more and more universities have opened up to the idea of shutting down classes for a week in the fall to relieve some of the stresses that go along with being a university student. Whether it is a myth or not the label of "suicide week" may have some validity to it as many students cannot cope with the first month and a half of university as the workload begins to pile up. In mid October, there are assignments that are in full swing and many students lack the proper work ethic and time management to get their work completed and more importantly completed on time. Throughout their high school years, this has never been something that was pressed upon them. They were never expected to get their work done on time or with any effort so when they enter university it is a complete shock to their system and they feel inundated with the pressure placed upon them. For some, the option to dropout is what they choose and for others they take a more drastic and terminal option of suicide. Whether the label "suicide week" is accurate or debunked, sadly it still occurs far too frequently than it should. If students were better prepared maybe less students would choose the suicide option.

"In Canada, suicide accounts for 24 percent of all death among 15-24 year olds. Suicide is the second leading cause of death for Canadians between the ages of 10 and 24" (Ontario.cmha). It is always tragic when a child dies and even more distressful when youth decide that their only option is to take their own life. Of all the deaths among 15-24 year olds the second leading cause of death among this age group is suicide. This number should not be so high. If students were properly prepared before entering university it would help lower the suicide rate. "Adolescence is a time of dramatic change. The journey from child to adult can be complex and challenging. Young people often feel tremendous pressure to succeed at school, at home and in social groups. At the same time, they may lack the life experience that lets them know that difficult situations will not last forever" (Canadiancrc). By treating school more like the 'real world' students would have an easier time adjusting to real world problems. "Due to strict classification rules, the number of teen suicides in Ontario could be significantly higher than official rate would indicate. We have cases in Ontario that would be classified as suicide in other areas that are classified as undetermined here, says Dr. David Eden" (thestar). As troubling as the number of cases of suicides is it is likely even higher than reported because how many actual suicides go unreported as such. Today's youth lack the understanding of how to deal with stress because they have not had to really deal with it. We need to teach our children to talk about their feeling when difficulty situations arise; we need to let them know that life is difficult at times and how to deal in certain situations. Parents, teachers and the education system on the whole does things to avoid hurting children's self-esteem, but yet in our avoidance of teaching them life skills we ignore the fact that life is not fair and bad things happen to good people which we should be preparing them for.

This continual ideological rhetoric of providing students opportunities for the best possible chance to be successful. We are forgetting important aspects that life does not conform—we have to conform to life and its intrinsic details. We make all sorts of changes under the guise of helping our youth but in the end what ends up happening is a total let down of future generations. The youth of today have plenty of distractions going on in their lives just like teenagers had twenty years ago, but we managed to survive. Conversely, the youth of today have technological devices to distract them like their cell phones, iPads, iPods, Facebook, Twitter to name a few. It is true the youth of twenty to thirty years ago did not have these devices but many more of them did have part time jobs that consumed their time while still maintaining a social life.

Unhealthy Living

Today, our youth are grossly unhealthy because of the sedentary lifestyle of video game consoles, games on their smartphones, texting and social media websites. The socializing that takes place now is largely through some form of technological device.

We as a society have conformed to our youth's lifestyle as so many of them refuse to get off their phones or their games to even get some sleep. This generation of youth are overly tired because they simply do not go to sleep. There is a lack of structure when children are not encouraged or forced to go to bed. Too many parents allow children to make decisions that they obviously are not ready to make because the choices they make are often the wrong ones. The idea of a fifteen year old going to bed at 2:00 am or later should never be acceptable. They need adequate sleep in order to function properly. These three or four hours of sleep per night is not working for them. We as adults must assert some modicum of authority over our children as opposed to permitting them to do as they want simply to avoid our youth's reign of terror. For the last number of years it has been the children who have asserted their dominance over us.

Common Sense is Not All That Common

There are numerous stories of children forcing their will onto their parent (s) someone either has their own stories or knows someone who has gone through some form of teenage terror. It baffles me that many children lack the mental capacity, responsibility and maturity to use an oven to cook for him or herself, yet are permitted to make life altering decisions that affect people around them. A number of years ago, a good friend of mine had the pleasure of dealing with her own child's reign of terror. At the time, her son was eleven years old and he did not like the particular rules that his mother had instituted in her home. As a single mother of two children she had the standard issue of caring for two children along with dealing with an ex who refused to pay child support. We see this all too often. She was working a full time job, raising two children on her own with absolutely no financial support while her children's father built up his financial nest egg at the expense of his children. As a result of certain rules, her eleven year old son decided to tell his teacher some outrageous story that his mother refused to let him in or out of the house. One day, he decided to get back at his mother for certain rules and hearing the word no—on occasion. He went to school and informed his teacher that he had to climb into his second floor bedroom window just to get into the house and go to sleep. In the morning he would have to climb out of the window in order to get to school. It is understood that teachers have a legal obligation to report any abuse that is going on with children. However, some common sense is needed in certain cases, such as this one, and maybe the teachers should have made a call home before contacting Children's Aid Society and starting an investigation of child abuse when it was clear that it was a fabricated story created by a young boy who did not like the rules.

Because common sense was not used, my friend was investigated and was made to feel that she was a horrible mother. This sort of thing happens far too often simply because some members of children's organization take their authority too far when common sense should prevail in situation as this one. Just like everything else we have gone too far the other way. I do not condone or advocate child abuse but when it is obvious there is no child abuse it should be called as it is and not pushed further because a child makes up obvious fictitious stories just to get his or her own way. Parents should be the authoritative figure in the household and not fear what their children will do if they do not like the rules set for them.

It is not just parents that are under constant scrutiny of their children. Teachers are also being falsely accused at an alarming rate. Mark Gollom of CBC News wrote an article discussing teachers being falsely accused. "Teachers across Canada are having their reputations ruined as an increasing number get falsely accused are on the rise. University of Ottawa faculty of Education professor, Joel Westheimer slammed school administrators for being spineless for automatically ordering investigations regardless of how credible the allegations of abuse may be" (CBC). We all know how children are these days and yet believe them over reputable professionals without even looking into the matter. It would take very little time and effort to properly question a student to get down to the truth. In the court of law it is innocent until proven guilty but in the court of public education it is the opposite of guilty until proven innocent. The sad state is once accused, it is nearly impossible to regain your name in the court of public opinion. "In one particular case, a teacher accused of physical assault committed suicide, even though he was cleared of the charges and the student recanted. While it may never be proven, his family (and many colleagues) share the view that [he] sought this drastic release because he could not bear the stain of a false accusation and the thought that his whole career was on the line" (CBC.ca). How many teachers will have to commit suicide or have their careers tarnished because of false accusations before the community of public opinion begins to investigate the allegations properly. It is not only teachers who have to deal with their reputation tarnished because of false accusations it also happens to parents. We all see how children behave and believe them without question and yet wonder why our youth are the way they are. We are constantly teaching our youth that misbehaving and not being honest is perfectly acceptable is today's world. When true abuse is taking place then it should be dealt with immediately and with the swiftness of manner to protect innocent children. However, let's make sure the story is absolutely truthful and accurate before we condemn innocent parents and teachers of inappropriate behaviour.

By allowing children to make life altering decisions we are intrinsically giving our youth the power that should be in the hands of parents and teachers. We make changes to mollify our youth and regardless what we do the majority of children just demand more. Such is the case for a Toronto high school when the decision to start classes an hour later to help with students' fatigue issues. Instead of moving school start times an hour later, parents should just tell their children to go to bed an hour earlier. Instead of changing the entire school structure to enable teens to continue their destructive ways. The role models in their lives should enforce some iota of parental discipline in their homes. "Aaron Best tries to ignore the buzzing that's ruining a perfectly good dream. Snuggled under the covers in his Scarborough bedroom, the 18—year-old Grade 12 students and star basketball player reluctantly open his eyes. Groggy from playing video games till after midnight—he was immersed in his favourite game, NBA 2K—he slaps the snooze button and drifts off for another 10 minutes. He hits the button three more times before he get out of bed at 7:30 am" (parentcentral.ca). As the article clearly states, Aaron Best was groggy from playing video games until past midnight. Maybe if he would have only played until 11 pm he would have more ease in getting up in the morning. In response to the lack of sleep that our youth receive, the school decided to push the start of school an hour later so there was less fatigue from the students. If they simply went to bed at a decent hour the issue of fatigue could be avoided

The report illustrates some positive aspects of starting school one hour later with grades improving slightly. In the short term, the pilot project appears to be successful, but what will be the long term affects? When the 10 am start becomes the norm, students will just expect it and then go to bed later because of their later start. What will take place after when the students going to bed later and still arrive at school late and extremely tired. Will schools implement an 11 am start to classes? Again, this is just another form of catering to our youth. What will happen when these same students go off to college, university or the workforce? How will they function when start times go back to 8 am or even 9 am? Will colleges or universities have to adjust their start times as well? Will they have to eliminate 8:30 classes altogether and avoid morning exams because our youth cannot function in the morning? Will the workforce be expected to push their start day later? Research was conducted in 2006 stating, "that North American teens are seriously sleep deprived. Noting that they need at least nine hours of sleep a night as their bodies grow, the poll found they were averaging just 6.9 hours. Sleep researcher Mary Carskadon who head the poll task force, says sleep deprivation seriously affects their ability to learn. But for many others, the late start just means more time for basketball practice. Typical is Samantha Prophet, 16, who, like her two siblings, enrolled in Eastern for the sport. She gets to school by 7:30 a.m. to practice, so the late start hasn't mean more sleep. And other still burn the candle at both ends, like Eliel Lukasa, who talks by cell to his friends and, also basketball mad, playing NBA 2K late at night. 'I'm always tired. I'll fall asleep in the weight room and go out cold for half an hour after lunch'" (parentcentral.ca). It is clear from the article that the late start does not instantly mean that students are getting more sleep as students are continuing to stay up late to play video games or to chat on their phones. It may help a few students but on the whole it does very little in terms of providing them the opportunity to attain class with more energy and wakefulness.

It is understood that not everyone can fall asleep at 10 p.m. in order to get the necessary sleep required but if they got in the routine of getting to bed with the purpose of turning off their phones to get much needed rest it would become routine and much easier to do. The problem is many students are glued to their phones and cannot turn it off or turn off the ringer and get some sleep. They have to respond to every text from all their friends regardless of the time of night and because of it they lack the necessary sleep. They need to learn to say goodnight to their friends and forget their phones so they can get some rest. If you want to upset a teenager do not respond to his or her text right away. They hate having to wait even 30 minutes for a text. That is why many stay up late because they are constantly getting text messages that they have to respond to instantly.

The argument that melatonin is what affects our sleep pattern is fine and that teenagers do not get tired at bedtime because of the chemicals within their bodies that won't allow them to sleep. Everyone was a teenager once and some teens were able to sleep. A few generations ago there were no cell phones to disrupt our sleep patterns and we did just fine. The argument that teens cannot sleep as a result of melatonin is highly suggestive and only makes excuses for the lack of sleep today's teens are getting. We have to stop making excuses for their behaviour. If the argument was supported over time, all teens would experience sleep deprivation and it was not always the case. Sleep deprivation today comes from the number of distractions that today's teens are faced with between the cell phones, their iPads, iPods and computers. Of course they do not want to sleep at night because they are inclined to be social and in this day of age socialization is taking over as the majority of youth from the age of twelve have cell phones. Their cell phones have become an extension of themselves. It is like their cell phone is a new appendage of their body. With the number of distractions that consume today's youth it is no wonder they cannot sleep when it is time to sleep. If their phones, iPods, computers were powered down more our youth would be able to sleep.

As a result of the lack of sleep our teens are becoming more and more exhausted and fail to stay coherent in class. In order t combat their exhaustion many teens turn to energy drinks. The issue with energy drinks is it helps revive them temporarily but then they feel a crash and need to drink more to alter the crash feeling. It is not uncommon for teens to be drinking 3 to 4 of these drinks per day. As a result of being hopped up on energy drinks all day long it plays havoc with their sleep patterns resulting in the inability to sleep at night. It becomes a vicious cycle they are tired so they need energy drinks to stay awake then they cannot sleep so they are up all night playing video games or texting so they get very little sleep. If the government really wanted to make a difference in the health issue in schools they should outlaw energy drinks in all schools across this province. Yes, it is true that school are no longer selling them but teens are simply going to stores and buying them and bringing them to school. If it was no longer permitted in school it would make a difference in helping them get back on track. In my classroom, my students know that they are not permitted to bring energy drinks in class. It is not the sole solution to getting kids some much needed rest but that in no way means the education system should continue to enable our students to further these bad habits in school. If they choose to drink them at home then that is up to their parent (s) to allow them or not we do not have to allow it in our schools. The health issue for our youth is horrendous as so many students eat unhealthy lunches if they eat at all. Many simply grab a bag of chips and an energy drink that is good enough for a lunch. A healthy lunch will make a difference in how our students are able to develop cognitive thinking and stay alert in class so they can be successful. Eating healthy is a good start to cognitive development and it should not be the school's responsibility to provide food to children.

It is obvious the world is changing depending on one's point of view it may be for the better or it might be for the worse. Whatever your point of view one thing that needs to be addressed is the direction of Ontario's education system and the perils it faces; if we do not take a stand against the known problems that is afflicting our current education system in Ontario the future will be a scary place. Just like everything else in our life we go from one extreme to the next. Back fifty years teachers and principals had all the power to do as they wish with their students and often times if the teacher or principal felt it necessary they would not think twice about striking a child. It began to improve slightly but even twenty-five years ago it was not uncommon for a child to be slapped by a teacher. I was slapped in the face twice, in one year, by the same teacher. When I went home and informed my mother of what happened she said, "You probably deserved it." I have never felt it was necessary or acceptable to inflict physical harm on a student. Consequently, because of all this Oprahfication of our youth the education system has gone too far on the opposite side and allows its students to lay some dominance and power over educators of this province. Far too often we hear of false claims against teachers and when it is uncovered to be a false claim there is little repercussions to the student (s) that make these allegations. It is simply a power struggle for students to show their dominance and authority over teachers for the sole reason because they can.

Teachers instil some modicum of authority in their classrooms at the beginning of the year or beginning of the semester; however, if the students do not buy into these particular rules they will simply refuse and the teacher has little power to enforce these class and school rules and students are fully aware of this. Because of this paradigm shift many excellent teachers are leaving the profession for health reasons as it has become too stressful to be a teacher in today's classrooms. Teachers lack the support needed to be effective educators. It comes to no surprise that cell phones and not permitted in the classroom for the obvious reason as they distract students in their learning process. They focus on their cell phones instead of the lesson that the teacher is conducting. However, cell phones always make their appearance and it has even gone as far as students answering their phones during class. In cases such as this what is a teacher to do? The teacher cannot remove the phone from the student because that would be borderline "abuse" or at least that is what students would claim. The only thing the teacher can do is tell the student to put their phone away and in doing so lends the idea of losing face in front of all other students. If a teacher does not inform the student to get off the phone and put it away then all other students have just witnessed the lack of authority the teacher actually has in their own classroom. If the teacher demands the students to get off the phone and the student refuses again the teacher loses face in front of the other students. When this happens, classroom management will become a complete disaster. The only power the teacher can exact is by sending that particular student to the office. Sending a disrespectful student to the office only shows how little authority and power the teacher has in the classroom because the only form of discipline that will take place is having someone else deal with the situation. How can an education system continue when teachers are left with so little disciplinary power in their own classroom? We need teachers to have the ability to put into effect their own way of managing their classroom for the benefit of the learning process. Ronald Morish wrote a wonderful book on classroom management that all teachers and parents should read. The book is called <u>With All Due Respect: Keys for Building Effective</u>

School Discipline. For classroom management to be truly effective in today's classrooms teachers and parents need to work together. Parents and teachers are stakeholders in the education that our students receive and both parties need to see eye-to-eye in such matters instead of being adversarial combatants.

It is understandable that this situation will not be fixed over night it will take some time and effort by all stakeholders and do so for the benefit of our youth, and our future. We need to get politics out of the classroom and educate for the sake of educating our youth so they can acquire the necessary knowledge that will help them become positive members of society. It is essential that we cease this downward spiral we are currently on for the benefit and well being as a society within this global world. There are numerous issues within our education system that needs readjusting it is not just one minor detail that is derailing our education system. I have discussed some problems that plague our educations system with the hopes of making necessary changes to improve the level of education Ontario's students receive in this fine province. It will not be all that fine for much longer if we continue down this path of apathy and melancholy. Our provincial government and our education leaders should reinvest their focus on our students as opposed to the political rhetoric that is all too consuming in the last decade or so. The education process should be more about our students then it is about trying to acquire votes and career ambitions. If the education was running effectively and efficiently the voting public would know and it would very well result in more votes for the political party in charge.

Our current education system in Ontario is going through a time of disillusionment of where our students are heading because of the lack of expectations placed upon them. We expect very little and in turn we get very little. The less we get the less we expect from them. It is a vicious cycle that needs to stop.

The issue that tends to get plenty of discussion in terms of where our education system is going is the financial side of it. The amount of cost that the government is forced to fund is what gets plenty of attention and I do agree no organization, business or social program should be hemorrhaging money. The government is always attempting to cut cost and at the moment the issue is amalgamating school boards to trim down $27 million dollars in the next two years. If administrative cuts need to be done to save money which does not affect the learning process then maybe that is what is needed. According to Near North District School Board's chairwoman Kathy Hewitt, "Students aren't any better off and schools suffer after amalgamations. It's not the best way to deliver services," Hewitt said. "It costs our director of education about $1,000 in wages and mileage to send him to Parry Sound for a day" (Nugget). A $1,000 a day to send the director of education from North Bay to Parry Sound? I do not understand where this number comes from as the director would be a salaried position so whether that person is in North Bay or travelling 90 minutes the wage would be the same. I do understand that gas prices are through the roof but it does not cost $1000 in gas to get from North Bay to Parry Sound. It is obvious there is plenty of wasteful spending going on if the cost to send the director of the board from North Bay to Parry Sound for one day would tally $1000.

However, the majority of the time the cuts that are being done are done to the frontline workers as in the teachers. If cuts are to be made it should be done at the EQAO level along with the numerous bureaucrats associated with the education system. There is plenty of waste; however it is not necessarily always with the teachers. There are numerous programs that cost the government money that could be scaled down if we just got back to teaching our students the way we used to. We need to get back to placing expectations on our students and when we do, I am confident they will reach them. When they do we will not need to amount of technological devices to do the work for them when they can do it for themselves. This Oprahfication mentality we as a society have with our youth may make them feel good because it provides them the idea of doing whatever they want that makes them feel good. Nevertheless it does nothing but teaches them bad habits and diminishes their work ethic and pride in what they do. Our youth simply do not care about anything besides their cell phone and whatever technological device they have. We have to get them to change their way of thinking earlier on to get them to care more than they do.

Conclusion

The common theme by people over 30 is that teenagers are completely rude and disrespectful which I am sure has been a common theme for the last 50 years. The situation we are in right now is not only are they rude and disrespectful they just do not care. The question that needs to be asked is why is this so? Yes, I do agree that many teens lack respect but we have to dig deeper and find out why this is the case because it appears much worse in the last decade then it has ever been. Our youth only know what they have been taught and what they have been taught is their lack of respect is not necessarily going unnoticed it is becoming almost acceptable in the grand scheme of things. If you allow a child to whine to get what he or she wants then they will whine to get what they want. Consequently, if you do not permit a child to whine then he or she will learn that whining does not work. This not only works for children it works for adults as well. If a woman finds out her husband has cheated and does nothing to stop this by accepting this behaviour and making excuses for it then her husband will continue to cheat. Why would he stop cheating if he can get away with it? This same concept works with everyone if we allow students to get away with their apathetic behaviours why would they stop?

Our education system should do more for students then just give them a place to be everyday and then after fourteen years we give them a piece of paper that states they put in a certain amount of time and effort into their academic learning to warrant this piece of paper. By allowing this behaviour to take place, students no longer see the education system as something of value because the people in charge of the education system do not place enough stock into it to elevate expectations. Regardless of the amount of expectations on students they clearly see there is very little value in their education because even when they do little to no work they are still successful. This type of thinking is extremely dangerous in devaluing our education system in Ontario and throughout North America for that matter. How can we expect students to place value on a system when their role models lack any real direction in how to run our education system? We clearly are confused about the direction and how we want to implement such policies because of the lack of leadership at the top of our education system. Our leaders are too short sighted because all that is important is the next few years—the political years. After that it will be someone else's responsibility someone else's problem.

With all that said, we need not to lay blame but take responsibility for our own part. Every stakeholder needs to take responsibility and make the necessary changes to improve our education system. The head of our system is not solely to blame but they are not innocent in all this as well. Board and school administrators need to look at themselves and what they have done to hurt the current education system. They need to forget all other school boards and what is going on over there and concentrate on their own schools and their own students. Administrators are not solely to blame and they too are not innocent in all this as well. Teachers to need to take responsibility and stop giving up because of what is going on at the top. They have to get back to teaching for the reason they entered the profession because they wanted to make a difference in the lives of our youth. Instead of being complacent because they feel a lack of support from administrators and parents they need to make a change. Parents who are the most important people in children's lives need to take responsibility for what they can do to give their children the proper start in their education. Parents who are apathetic towards education teach their children that education is not all that important and thus leads to students' apathy towards their own learning experience. When all stakeholders do their part, the students themselves will follow because when they have proper leadership they will understand what is needed and what is expected of them.

In the sports world when an organization does poorly for a certain length of time the management team must make a change otherwise they risk losing their own jobs. Sometimes it means firing the head coach with the hopes that a new coach can right the ship. Sometimes coaching changes do not work so the general manager makes roster changes and completes a few trades. On occasion, ownership decides that the general manager's position needs to be changed for the team to head into a new direction. Sometimes the organization has to start fresh and go with new management, coaches and make a plethora of roster moves. There are times where the team has to blow things up (figuratively speaking) and rebuild the team anew to get back on the winning track. Something the Toronto Maple Leafs should consider. By the way it looks the direction of our education system is in a similar position and is in need of a rebuild. We need change to take place and it needs to be done right away. Our children's future is at stake. The education system in this province needs to be revamped in order to make the learning process much more adaptable for our students. This current system is not working. We need real change and not just change for the sake of change. If Ontario's children are ever going to compete in the global world our education system needs to provide them with the tools to be successful in the future. We all need to stand up and demand better for ourselves and for our children. We do not need to lay blame we need to all take responsibility for our part in this atrophy of our education system.

I feel strongly about the teaching profession and the youth of this province and for that reason it is vital that changes be made to provide the necessary steps to prepared Ontario's students for their future. We all want what is best for our children sometimes the ideas of assisting our children get skewed and we lose touch with how to get there. What I suggest is we need to find a happy medium or a common goal to satisfy all parties to attain what is in the best interest of Ontario's youth. Allowing children to hold parents and teachers hostage is not a way to move into the future. To acquiesce to the current behaviour is doing more harm to Ontario's youth then showing our children some discipline and taking responsibility for them by setting rules and expecting them to follow the rules. "There is a 100 percent guarantee that nothing will change if you don't step up. What's more, we are much more likely to regret having stayed on the sidelines that we are to regret our failures" (Izzo, 33). We as an enlightened society have to step up and make changes to the current education system because whatever we do cannot make things worse than they are right now. There are not many people that will truly believe that the current situation is heading in the right direction. The only people that may would be the same people who continue to make the situation worse. We need to step up and do it for Ontario's youth and for Ontario's future. The youth of today are the leaders of tomorrow. As it stands right now are you confident with our future?

Resources

Izzo, John Ph.D. <u>Stepping Up: How Taking Responsibility Changes Everything.</u> San Francisco: Berrett-Koehler Publishers, Inc. 2012. http://www.eqao.com/

Morrish, Ronald G. <u>With All Due Respect: Keys for building effective school discipline.</u> Fonthill: Woodstream Publishing. 2000.

Works Cited

Baluja, Tamara. "iPads are in, cursive is out (and other educational trends)." *Globe and Mail.* Nov. 30 2011. http://www.theglobeandmail.com/news/national/education/primary-to—secondary/ipads-are-in-cursive-is-out-and-other-education-trends/article2254353/.

"Building the Ontario Education Advantage: Student Achievement." Apr. 2004. < www.edu.gov.on.ca>.

<http://www.canadiancrc.com/Youth_Suicide_in_Canada.aspx>.

Casey, Liam & Hunter, Paul. "Suicide may be underreported in Ontario." *Thestar.com.* Dec. 2011.

<http://www.thestar.com/news/article/1096529—suicide-may-be-substantially-underreported-in-Ontario>.

<http://www.edu.gov.on.ca/eng/document/nr/04.03/building.pdf>.

<http://www.eqao.com/>.

Gollom, Mark. "False abuse accusations against teachers 'on the rise'." *CBC News.* Apr. 24, 2012 http://www.cbc.ca/news/canada/story/2012/04/23/teachers-falsely-accused.html.

"Growing Success: Assessment, Evaluation and Reporting in Ontario Schools" 2010. <http://www.edu.gov.on.ca/eng/policyfunding/growSuccess.pdf>.

Hamilton-McCharles, Jennifer. "School boards concerned about possible amalgamations." *North Bay Nugget* June 2012. < http://www.nugget.ca/ArticleDisplay.aspx?e=3571364>.

Inderawati, Rita & Hayati, Rita. "Short-term Training Model of Academic Writing to High School Teachers." Aug. 2011. < http://davidpublishing.org/journals_show_abstract.html?3977-0>.

Izzo, John Ph.D. Stepping Up: How Taking Responsibility Changes Everything. San Francisco: Berrett-Koehler Publishers, Inc. 2012.

<http://www.learningandteaching.info/learning/piaget.htm>.

Loriggio, Paola. "Mid-term interventions reduce university drop-out rates." *Globe and Mail.* Oct. 2011. <http://economics.uwo.ca/centres/cibc/pressreferences/postsecondary/Stinebrickner_GlobeandMail_Oct30_2011.pdf>.

Mali, Taylor. "The the Impotence of Proofreading" <http://taylormali.com/poems-online/the-the-impotence-of-proofreading/>.

<http://www.maritamoll.ca/webmom/costs.html>.

McLeod, Saul. "Vygotsky." *Simply Psychology.* 2007. <http://www.simplypsychology.org/vygotsky.html>.

O'Brien, Jennifer. "Principal suspended with pay." Lfpress.com. Nov. 2010. <http://www.lfpress.com/news/london/2010/11/17/16186206.html>.

<http://www.ontario.ca/en/initiatives/progressreport2011/ONT05_039131.html?openNav=education>.

<http://www.ontario.cmha.ca/fact_sheets.asp?cID=3965>.

<http://www.parentcentral.ca/parent/education/post-secondary/article/923380—toronto-school-starts—hour-later-and-grades-improve>.

Peterson, Jordan B. & Mar, Raymond. "The Benefits of Writing." <http://www.selfauthoring.com/WritingBenefits.pdf>.

Reynolds, Cynthia. Why your teenager can't use a hammer." *MacLean's. ca* Aug. 25, 2011. <http://www2.macleans.ca/2011/08//25/why-your-teenager-cant-use-a-hammer/>.

"Universities try to curb dropout rates." *CTV News.* Sept. 26, 2010. <http://toronto.ctvnews.ca/universities-try-to-curb-dropout-rates-1.556848>.

"Vygotsky's Theory of Child Development." <http://www.ethicalpolitics.org/wits/vygotsky-development.pdf>.

Wilhelm, Jeffrey PH.D. Improving Comprehension with Think-Aloud Strategies. New York: Scholastic, 2001.

Zinkosky, Pamela. "K-12 Grades: How Writing Benefits Students." <http://www.eduguide.org/library/viewarticle/273/>.

www.ingramcontent.com/pod-product-compliance
Lightning Source LLC
LaVergne TN
LVHW042336060326
832902LV00006B/215